A WALK

Through

TEARS

By Dot Roberts With
Dr. Ricky Roberts

CREATION
HOUSE PRESS
A STRANG COMPANY

A WALK THROUGH TEARS by Dot Roberts
    with Dr. Ricky Roberts
Published by Creation House Press
A Strang Company
600 Rinehart Road
Lake Mary, FL 32746
www.creationhouse.com

Unless otherwise noted, the Scripture quotations are from The King James Version of the Bible.

Scripture quotations marked NKJV are from the New King James Version of the Bible. Copyright © 1979, 1980, 1982 by Thomas Nelson, Inc., publishers. Used by permission.

Cover design by Kirk Douponce
Interior design by David Bilby

Library of Congress Control Number: 2003105731
International Standard Book Number: 1-59185-236-6

This book was previously published by Dr. Ricky Roberts, ISBN 0-8187-0347-4, copyright © 2001.

03 04 05 06   8 7 6 5 4 3 2 1

Printed in the United States of America

*To all those who are without hope
and dare to seek after the God
of the miraculous.*

Acknowledgments

We acknowledge all those who have helped us in this endeavor and all those who have given testimony to this miracle. We especially thank University Christian School for their permission to use the photographs illustrating that Dr. Ricky Roberts was in a special education class and was classified as mentally disabled at one time. We thank also those who helped in the proofreading of this manuscript.

Contents

Foreword

By a Healed Dr. Ricky Roberts

This book chronicles the life, suffering and progress through many years of struggle against the attacks of Satan who battled to keep me enslaved to a diagnosis of mental retardation. My complete healing is the result of many tears and cries to Almighty God on my behalf that are found in the pages of this book.

The purpose of this book is not for my mother to recount the complete history of my life as a retarded person. Being a Ph.D., I could have easily written that book with a higher level of comprehension. I saw from the very beginning that the true purpose of this book was to focus on the miraculous background leading to the miracle itself, the cost of gaining such an amazing miracle from God and the miracle's aftermath. This book needed to be written by the one who cried bitterly for my healing more than all others, my mother. I am honoring her faith, her life and her struggle for my healing. If she had not stood in the gap for me, I may never have been healed. Indeed, I may have even totally succumbed to the devices of Satan.

By looking at the outer person, we cannot realize the struggle and hurt that he or she has inwardly endured. My mother has suffered many combat wounds from fighting fiercely on my behalf. Instead of praising her battle for her retarded son, many people seem to envy my healing or feel jealous about the miracle that she gained. They do not realize that what God did through her can be done through all willing vessels. There is a great cost to be paid, however. My mother did not let the emotions, thoughts and ideas of others stop her from pushing forward to touch the hem of Jesus' garment. She was willing to pay the cost of stretching out to touch the Master's robe so that her retarded child could be healed from disability. What was the cost that she was willing to pay? She paid the cost of being an intercessor, putting God first above all else and giving Him everything.

I am able to write this forward as a thankful servant of the Most High God who has been healed from retardation because my mother touched the heart of Almighty God. I can say nothing about my healing in any sense, except that it was an awesome act of grace. I am speechless and overwhelmed by the mercy of God in my life. Out of the approximately fifty students in University Christian's special education class over the years, upon only one did God's grace fall in such a manner as to heal him of retardation. I am that person and my healing is for the glory of God alone!

This awesome act of love that saved me from a state of hopelessness is almost indescribable. I would not wish upon anyone the curse that I experienced as a mentally challenged individual—the laughter, jokes, funny looks, dislike and embarrassment that were the norm of my life.

As a person restored, I cry bitter tears over all those children and adults who have not been set free from their handicap. I seek God for their deliverance and pray that someone will touch the hem of His garment for them!

Ancient civilizations considered retardation (like seizures) an affliction from the gods. To me, the only word that can describe retardation in all its disguises is the word *curse*. I don't feel that being mentally challenged was a state of blessing for me; those who say that it is have never lived with it. If they could experience for one moment the effects of such an affliction, they would take back these sentiments. How can a life of retardation be a blessing? I do know that I would never want that "blessing" back! Since God healed me from that affliction twenty-three years ago, I have not missed a day of that adversity. I can now live in freedom, because of my deliverance by a mighty and merciful God.

A mental disability destroys all elements of time, space and dignity within a person's life. If God does not move to prevent it, all hope, promise and life can also be obliterated. There is no recollection of responsibility within a retarded person's life, leaving emptiness of mind and sometimes body. As a retarded person, I felt no glimmer of hope or promise without God.

It is this miserable state that has left many to believe the retarded are less than human. This evil philosophy, espoused by Nazi Germany, pushed for the killing of the retarded during World War II. It is also this outlook that helps promote the murdering of the unborn today through abortion.

Given the morals of today's society, perhaps I would have been aborted to rescue society from an unwanted burden. Think about it! If I had been aborted, I would never have suffered the horror of retardation. But God would have been robbed of a miracle. Retardation is not God's fault but our own! I don't attribute my retardation to God. Instead I point to the sin of man as its root cause.

As a disabled person, I lived in my own little world. In my early years I did not worry about how my life would be as an adult. The retardation blinded me from realizing the hopelessness I would face as an adult if God did not heal me.

If it were possible for embarrassment to kill, it would have murdered me countless times. My whole life as a retarded child was filled with embarrassment. I was self-conscious about learning, living, walking, eating, talking, my weight, and my inability to read, have friends and express myself as God intended. In essence, the first sixteen years of my life can best be described as a Greek Tragedy: When hope would surface for a partially normal life, disappointment and disaster would raise their ugly heads and destroy it. No peace was there!

My life as a retarded person was such that I had to pay to have friends. I always felt alone, even in the midst of a crowd—an outcast, never fitting in anywhere—a broken vessel, thrown away by the world, through Satan's devices. In essence I saw myself as the worst of the worst and the most miserable of the miserable. During all the time of my retardation, I can remember little happiness and no real life. I was physically breathing, yet there was no vitality to my emotions, thoughts or mind. My spirit was normal and cried out for healing from God even though my mind was traumatized by the state of retardation.

I can recall the many times in which I found myself pretending to read even though I could not recognize a single word. At the barbershop I would pretend to read magazines even though the only things I really comprehended were the pictures. In the midst of my retardation, I became fearful of all books but the Bible. This seemed to be my Waterloo, where I would go down in total defeat. God, through His grace, changed what I thought was my downfall into my victory, by healing my retardation.

Since God has allowed me to retain the memories of my retardation, I can easily recall the times in which I was called "retarded," "stupid," "idiot" and "moron." Untold harm and hurt resulted from these words being spoken. I realize now that they were spoken out of ignorance and fear: Many people are uneasy about what is abnormal and often express it as hatred. Since my mind was affected rather than my spirit, the meaning of all these words was filtered through my spirit, and I sought after the God of the miraculous, crying out to Him for assistance. It was my spirit that said, "Forgive them, for they know not what they do!"

Even now, I must admit that some church people look at me as an outcast or somewhat strange. They seem unable to grasp the scope of the miraculous that touched my life. They are satisfied with living their lives, not realizing how much more that God could do if they allowed Him.

In some circles criticism against me is common, denouncing my higher education as useless. While I was working on my degree, a man prophesied that it was not God's will for me to study ancient languages and continue my college education. I am so thankful that I know His voice and His written Word! That prophecy was not in agreement with God's written Word. How could I be able to go to college, study languages and receive advanced degrees? It was not because of my own ability and capacity! All of these things came because of the grace of God shining upon my life in a miraculous way.

As the reader will discover, the aftermath of such an awesome act of grace continues. I have been led in many ways as God has directed; not only was I led to go to college, but I was also directed to study ancient languages and theology. God then guided me to form a ministry. All of this came through someone who could not comprehend or understand any of these things by his own ability. God's miracle of grace is that He can take that which is considered useless and turn it into a miracle of His design and purpose.

In March of 1999, I founded a nondenominational ministry known as "True Light Ministries," based upon 1 John 2:8. Its purpose is defined as: "We follow the 'Old Way' already trodden down by the early church in its first three hundred years and follow their landmarks back to the cross and back to the original Christian faith. We seek to study the Word of God in the original languages and to understand that what was taught was, in fact, what the early church taught."

Since the founding of this ministry, more than two thousand confirmed healings, miracles and deliverances have taken place. More than two hundred prophecies have been fulfilled in less than two years. There have also been several manifestations of golden flakes, fulfilling Psalms 68:13. Many have experienced countless signs of flowing oil upon walls, windows and foreheads of people. This fulfills Zechariah 4:14, and confirms the belief in the fresh oil which represents fresh anointing.

There was one manifestation of the oil that I

will never forget. I had forgotten my own bottle of oil and had to borrow one with very little liquid in it. I said, "God will provide the oil we need." As I was teaching the Word of God, oil multiplied within the bottle and its color changed to a cloudy white. Everyone present saw this sign and wonder. I continued to teach God's Word. When I ended my instruction, I lifted up the bottle and took off the top. The most wonderful fragrance filled the church. Under the direction of the Lord, I tasted the oil. Its taste was that of a very expensive perfume. This manifestation took place in Alma, Georgia, in the year 2000, when I was thirty-eight years old and teaching on the last days. The oil was to be used to anoint people for prayer in accordance with James 5:13–18 and Mark 6:13.

I firmly believe that someone else was originally called to take on this ministry and to experience these manifestations of the Spirit. I also believe that this same person rejected his or her calling and election, causing God to look for one who would obey Him and do as He directed. As God looked upon a retarded teenager, He saw a hopeless life and a broken vessel that the world would never accept. God chose the foolish things to confound the wise and the world. (See 1 Corinthians 1:27.) He chose me, that broken instrument, having nothing to lose and everything to gain. I owe God my all: my ability, capacity, understanding, comprehension, mind, ministry, manifestations of the Spirit and health.

I deserved none of these things then and do not deserve them now.

Soon after I was healed, the Lord Himself told me two very important things that have been burned into my consciousness. The first was, "Ricky, if you forget everything that I ever told you, forget not that the One who giveth can taketh away." The second one was, "Ricky, I will never, as long as you live, take away from you the memories of your retardation. They will remain in your mind as a memorial unto where I have brought you from."

I praise God that He healed a retarded teenager for His glory, His grace and the coming Great Awakening.

VERBUM IPSE DEUS

Introduction

By a Healed Dr. Ricky Roberts

L ong before the dawn of the Reformation, a holy saint of God made a powerful statement. His name was Tertullian and he was a leader of the church in the third century. His statement rocks the very foundation of modern theologies and all the theologies fashioned since the Reformation. In dealing with the apostate Marcion, who defected from the early church, Tertullian said:

> Consequently, it will be clearly seen of what the apostle speaks, even of those things that were to happen in the church of his God; as long as He endures, so long also does His Spirit work, and so long are His promises repeated.[1]

What force there is in Tertullian's argument! Those who deny the continuation of the supernatural gifts so deny the continuation of God enduring and the Holy Spirit still working.

The history of the church is filled with the manifestations of the Holy Spirit. Remove those manifestations and church history is not only

1

incomplete, but also lifeless. Christianity without these supernatural manifestations of the Holy Spirit is nothing more than a dead religion and a dead hope. Miracles are what distinguish Christianity from simple theism. History proves that these signs were not counterfeit as some people may imagine.

The early church and revivalists like John Wesley, all dogmatically taught that the supernatural gifts of the Holy Spirit and their outward manifestations had not yet ceased. When Reverend Middleton declared that the gifts and their manifestations had been withdrawn, Wesley cried out, "O Sir, mention this no more. I entreat you, never name their silence again. They speak loud enough to shame you as long as you live."[2]

In the Great Awakening, headed by Jonathan Edwards, there were many manifestations of the Holy Spirit. Some voiced such concern about these supernatural gifts and their manifestations that they accused the entire Great Awakening Movement of being in league with Satan. Jonathan Edwards refuted those accusations and preached on the genuine and counterfeit signs, affirming that what had occurred in the Great Awakening was genuine. Indeed, Jonathan Edwards concluded that God could still perform miracles, speak to His people, show dreams and visions and work all sorts of other manifestations.

In his writings, Edwards describes many persons who, in his day, were the subjects of the extraordinary work of the Holy Spirit. He describes one person who continued for five or six hours in a vision of Christ. When the vision ended, the person thought that only a minute had passed. Extraordinary views of divine things such as prophecy, tongues and the like manifested themselves frequently in this revival. Some people for a time could neither stand nor speak. Others experienced their hands clenched and their flesh cold while their senses remained intact. Some shook uncontrollably and fell to the ground. An extraordinary sense of the awesome majesty, greatness and holiness of God overwhelmed the soul and body of all that witnessed these manifestations of the Spirit, and a sense of repentance filled the whole revival.

On the continuation of the supernatural gifts of the Holy Spirit and their manifestations, Edwards confesses, "The whole tenor of the Gospel proves it; all the notion of religion that the Scripture gives us confirms it."[3] In his work entitled, *Mark of a Work of the True Spirit*, he says that the Holy Spirit, "has brought to pass new things, strange works, and has wrought enough to surprise both men and angels. As God has done thus in times past, so we have no reason to think but that He will do so still."[4]

Did not Paul himself say that the gospel of Christ was fulfilled in His ministry through mighty signs and wonders by the power of the Spirit of God? (See Romans 15:19.) Without the manifestations of the Holy Spirit, the gospel cannot be fulfilled. No wonder the early church said that the gospel of the apostles was truly full and that the apostles and their disciples taught the "full Gospel." The failure of the church at large today is due in great part to its rejection of the Holy Spirit, His gifts and the manifestations of these gifts in the church. The church has failed to give the Holy Spirit His rightful place.

This book is about the miracles of God still being alive and well. It is about the miraculous act of God when faith is not blinded or weakened but looks into the realm of the impossible for God's assistance. It is about believing that God's Spirit will work as long as He endures. It is about proclaiming to a child that God is still a God of the miraculous and telling him or her to reach out to that God. It is a witness that in the craziness of this world, God still performs miracles and healings. It is a proclamation to all the saints to retain their faith, no matter what happens. It is an exhortation to stand strong, no matter what opposition Satan puts one through. It is a vindication that, along with the angels, *Our God liveth*!

Miracles and healings of all sorts are the bread of the saints. (See Matthew 15:26.) They are indications that God is alive and well upon this planet and that the Word of God has been and continues to be sustained, substantiated and proven. These manifestations of the Spirit bring freedom since the Lord is there and working before the people. (See Isaiah 61:1.) Did not Paul himself say, "Where the Spirit of the Lord is, there is liberty"? (See 2 Corinthians 3:17.) How does the Holy Spirit bring liberty? He brings it through His supernatural manifestations, whatever they may be.

The belief that God is still the God of the miraculous is our only hope when the storms of life are raging and times of suffering leave us gasping. This belief is often sparked by God's promise (whether from the Scriptures themselves or through a word given) that He will move and perform the miraculous in our lives. That belief becomes a pillar and a foundation that cannot be toppled by the pounding waters of Satan's oppression. We can stand like Daniel, still looking to the God of the miraculous, with an assurance beyond this realm that God will move and rescue us. We need to continue to hold on to Him by meeting, keeping and fulfilling His conditions, no matter what happens.

Our life was so ravaged by suffering that no peace or rest penetrated our lives. Many times as my mother would drive to work, she would cry out to God for death. The storms began before I was born and continued for over thirty years. Only now are we experiencing peace and rest in our lives. St. Paul said that in order to reign with Christ, we must suffer. (See 2 Timothy 2:12.) My family and I are living witnesses to this Scripture. Satan often tried to destroy the lives of my father, my mother and me. He sought to prevent God's intentions and purposes for our lives and might have succeeded if my father and mother had not held on to believing God above everything else.

It is important to remember that Paul saw the state of suffering and the state of grace joined as one whole. 1 Peter 5:10 reminds us that the victorious Christian can only be seen through the state of suffering. By yielding to this suffering, we will learn humility and reverence. (See Romans 12:12.)

It was during these times of great suffering that my mother cried many bitter tears over my life of retardation. It was at this time that God placed her tears into a bottle as a memorial of God's grace that would be poured out upon me. Remember David! David said, "Put thou my tears into thy bottle." (See Psalms 56:8.)

She learned the meaning of this expression while going through the pain. "O eyes, no eyes, but fountains fraught with tears! O Life, no life, but lively form of death!"[5] It was then that she knew, "out of the presses of pain cometh the soul's best wine and the eyes, which shed no tears, can shed but little shine and glory!"[6]

I am convinced that her tears reached the very heart of God. These tears became the backbone of the ministry that was to come forth. Her tears nourished this ministry and gave birth to it. It was prophesied, "Every tear that she sowed in prayer was a seed which the Lord received that will bring forth a million-fold blessing and harvest that God will produce in the ministry!" Tertullian once said that the blood of the martyrs nourished the church. My ministry and life have been nourished in the same way by the tears of my mother. The Psalmist said, "They that sow in tears shall reap in joy. He that goeth forth and weepeth, bearing precious seed, shall doubtless come again with rejoicing, bringing his sheaves with him." (See Psalms 126:5–6.)

Tears, deep feeling and emotion are important parts of prayer. Emotional experiences often move us to pray. Many times tears are the visible sign that God is working in us. They seem to refresh the very working of our spirits. Tears can be seen as mirror images of our very beings. It can well be said that they contain our thoughts, feelings, memories, failures and successes. They also symbolize the surrendering of ourselves to God. (See Psalms 42:3; 56:8; 126:5; Acts 20:19; 2 Kings 20:5.)

When God speaks to us, we often anticipate Him working at warp speed to accomplish what He has promised. The problem is that God does not always work as fast as we want Him to work. Sometimes He delays to test our faith. When this happens, we must stand firmly, holding on when there is no hope. We need to be like the patriarchs and other saints of the Old Testament who believed and held on whether they received their promise or not. (See Hebrews 11:1–13.)

A. W. Tozer once said, "The Bible was written in tears and to tears it will yield its best treasure."[7] The Bible may be said to be "a theology of tears." It was the tears of Hezekiah that touched God and moved God to heal him. (See 2 Kings

20:1.) Notice that Hezekiah mixed his prayers with tears and found acceptance. David said that his tears were his meat day and night. (See Psalms 42:3.)

God views tears as a sign of trust. They symbolize that we trust Him for our home, our lives and all our possessions. God sees tears as a glorious sign that we are surrendering to Him. They are the bursting forth of total surrender to a merciful God.

The ministries of the prophets and the apostles were founded upon their tears. Their weeping affected what they thundered in words. Their cries reached the throne of God and He granted them assistance and commissioned them for mission.

The early saints saw tears as a sign of repentance and a cleansing agent of the Lord. The tears of the woman who cried out for Jesus were a sign of her repentance and sorrow. (See Matthew 26:7–13.) These same believers beseeched the Lord in travail and repentance. They believed that lamentation and tears could touch the heart of God when nothing else could. These men and women understood that God saw Hezekiah's tears and was moved to extend his life. (See 2 Kings 20:1.) When two or more saints shed tears over a believer, Christ also sheds tears and prays for mercy. God is satisfied with faithful tears that are shed from eyes that have looked upon wickedness. Tears are sent forth as ambassadors to God to relay our sufferings.

The Jews believed that the tears of the Jewish women touched God so much that He caused Pharaoh to set the Jewish nation free. These tears turned God's face toward the Jewish people rather than turning it away because of their sin. The tears of the women touched God deeply.

My mother often said that she believed that she cried a river of tears stretching from Jacksonville to Fernandina, Florida. Her commuting time to work became her prayer time. While experiencing these bitter tears, my mother would wonder if God had forsaken us. She sometimes questioned God's presence with us. But He was always there, right in the midst of the storms, never forsaking or abandoning us. (See Hebrews 13:5.)

God's promises are utterly reliable and dependable. God cannot lie! He has never left us even if he sometimes seems far away. Deliverance will come, but it may take longer than we want. Redemption comes in God's timing, not our own. (See Ecclesiastes 3; Psalms 34:19.) If we forget that and blame God for our failures, we bring destruction upon our lives.

Even David himself said in Psalm 22:1, "My God, my God, why hast thou forsaken me?" This verse teaches us that there are many times when suffering causes us to think that we are alone, without God and His love.

A nineteenth century poet, Frederick W. Faber, expressed so eloquently this seeming absence of God in times of trouble: [8]

He hides Himself so wondrously
As though there were no God;
He is least seen when all the powers
of ill are most abroad.
Or He deserts us at the hour
The fight is almost lost.
And seems to leave us to ourselves
Just when we need Him most
It is not so, but so it looks;
And we lose courage then;
And doubts will come if God hath kept
His promise to men.

Someone once said, "God is not the God over troubled waters but the God through troubled waters." It is God who carries us through the storms of life. He showers us with blessings and delivers us after the storms of life blow over. God will pull us through but we have to be able to withstand His grip. This pulling often can bring pain and anguish because we do not understand what God wants. But we can gain the victory over the turbulence if we learn to be more like Christ. The philosophy of the cross is, "We must decrease and He must increase."

Cry out to the God of the miraculous as our whole family did. Beseech Him to touch those who seem untouchable or appear to have no hope. God is the God of the hopeless as is evidenced by my life. Without Him, there was no hope for me. Our family motto became: "We would rather believe and not receive than could have believed and could have received." We held on by not giving in, not giving up and not giving out. The promises that God made in His Word regarding healing and miracles became our victory cry. We had simple and uneducated faith that these promises were valid and we did whatever God demanded of us. What God desires most is that we reach up to Him so that He can reach down to us!

Chapter One

BEGINNINGS
OF A MIRACLE

My husband, George Elias Roberts, and I were raised just twenty miles apart from each other. Both our fathers worked as farmers during the Great Depression.

My husband was born prematurely and was not supposed to live. There was little in the way of hospital care, money or proper equipment to handle a baby born so early. He was so small that the family related that "his bed was a shoe box." His sister remembers that his mother's wedding ring could slide up his arm to the elbow. Because of this premature birth, he had to be watched twenty-four hours a day, kept at a very warm temperature and fed with an eyedropper. These circumstances were difficult because the house that the family lived in was old, cold and drafty with many holes in the walls and a sole fireplace as the only heat.

Since almost everyone around Coffee County, Georgia, had lost their possessions during the Great Depression, a family was fortunate to have food on the table and a place to live. A doctor was positively a luxury. Any town lucky enough to have a doctor usually paid him with bacon, ham or chickens. Since these were very dear, most of the poor families used old medicinal remedies to treat illness instead.

The circumstances of those difficult times were no different for Elias, though it helped that his grandmother Lanie was a midwife. In the course of her work she had seen so many premature babies die and knew that her grandson would need a miracle to survive. In addition to being a prayer warrior, Grandmother Lanie was also a jack-of-all-trades. She was a midwife, intercessor, and a retailer selling eggs and other things grown on the farm. She could do a little preaching, too! She was the one who taught my mother-in-law how to pray.

Many godly men and women living in the Great Depression found time to pray all night. They also made it a point to fast during these hard times. Though many had lost most of their worldly possessions, their faith and time with God never lessened. In fact, the hard times made them stronger in their faith even while others were undergoing financial and spiritual collapse all around. Many became shipwrecked in their faith while others, by the grace of God, found their faith. These people persevered in their faith by never giving in, never giving up and never giving out.

Elias was very sickly for most of his life. He

described having the worst "swimming headaches" as a young child. These types of headaches are similar to migraines but with some medical differences. Elias often talked about carrying water in a bucket to his father in the field and having these headaches begin. When this took place, he would actually see the field turning around and would often vomit. He was unable to hold up his head and would have to be carried back to the house.

Thank God for praying saints! The family had a neighbor known as "Jumping Jim Carter" who had an ice route. One day Jim Carter found Elias sick with one of his headaches when he came to deliver ice. Mrs. Roberts asked Brother Carter if he had time to pray for Elias. His answer was, "I always have time to pray for someone who's sick." After Brother Carter prayed for Elias, his swimming headaches completely disappeared.

God's infinite mercy touched Elias and delivered him from those horrible headaches through Brother Carter's prayer. Fifty years later God allowed Elias to be instrumental in laying the foundation for Brother Carter's great-great-grandson to be saved.

So often Satan tried his best to see that Elias was killed or injured. When he was seven or eight years old, his oldest brother, J. H., carried him down to a water hole to go swimming. Elias jumped in and landed on a log underneath the water, causing severe damage and pain to his lower back. The damage and pain were so bad that J. H. thought that Elias was dead and had broken his back. It took some time before Elias could walk again. The pain never left him even though God healed him of many illnesses and injuries after that. Yet, Elias never allowed this pain to get the better of him. Many days he worked tirelessly despite the pain to provide for our family.

As Charles Dickens once said, "It was the best of times; it was the worst of times." Our parents did not think that education was important. They taught us how to work and thought that was the only education that we needed. Dealing with this attitude of prejudice against education forced Elias to remain uneducated, keeping him tied to farm work as a means to make a living. Although his formal education extended only through the third grade, he had a head full of common sense. However, Satan deprived him of the opportunity to study and be well rounded. We will never know what might have happened if people then had been more versed in spiritual warfare. Maybe more would have opposed Satan's plans and devices.

Remember what Jesus said about Satan and later about Himself? "The thief cometh not, but for to steal, and to kill, and to destroy; I am come that they might have life, and that they might have it more abundantly." (See John 10:10.) Notice that Christ says here that the saints can have life more abundantly. In Elias' early life, Satan stole many things from him due to a lack of knowledge rather than the presence of sin. No one in that area was teaching the Word of God as it should be taught. Friends and family were unable to attend church regularly so that they could learn the means to fight Satan. Going to church involved either a mule-drawn wagon or a late night walk through the woods. Their concern was not so much about how to fight Satan as it was how to survive.

The Word of God says, "My people are destroyed for lack of knowledge: because thou has rejected knowledge, I will also reject thee, that thou shalt be no priest to me: seeing thou hast forgotten the law of thy God, I will also forget thy children." (See Hosea 4:6.) The rejection of knowledge, especially godly knowledge, destroys people. Wisdom, and a well-rounded education that is grounded upon the Word of God, will bring life and deliverance.

Satan repeatedly wins by deception and ignorance. Paul himself said, "Lest Satan should get an advantage of us: for we are not ignorant of his devices." (See 2 Corinthians 2:11.) We can learn how Satan operates through our study of the Scriptures, the Holy Spirit and our experience. We must not be ignorant of Satan and his devices. When we're uninformed, we reap nothing but evil and destruction. We need to realize that as soon as one battle ends, another begins. The Christian walk is filled with battles ending and battles beginning, because Satan never gives up fighting against a saint.

Despite the limitation of his environment, Elias was able to hold down jobs. In fact, he worked for forty-one years operating a machine that makes cardboard boxes for two different companies. God gave him the ability to listen to the corrugator machine running and, just by listening, to diagnose what was wrong with it. For this talent he was named, "Mister Corrugator of America." He was offered a job with a large company that involved traveling about the country, installing corrugators and teaching others how to use this very large machine. Because he knew that I could not raise our retarded son Ricky alone, he had to turn down this wonderful job opportunity. Yet, he did not regret rejecting this offer. His son and our family were more important to him than anything in the world. From the time that Ricky was born until he was six years old, he slept in our bed under Elias' arm. If Ricky had a convulsion while we were sleeping, Elias would know immediately what was wrong. He would often wake me up to get a spoon to put on Ricky's tongue. If this happened we knew that we were on the way to the hospital again.

Elias was the kind of man who was unselfish, putting his child before everything but his relationship with the Lord. He was always willing to get up and cook something for Ricky to eat if he became hungry during the night. Because of Ricky's sickly disposition, whenever he wanted something to eat, we gave it to him. To us, Ricky's hunger was a sign that he was all right.

Elias was never too tired to carry Ricky to kindergarten or to a tutor. He also was willing to cook, wash and take care of Ricky for me when I had to work. He was familiar with the working of the house and relieved me of much responsibility. Some of the best times that I remember were when we cooked, gardened and canned fresh vegetables together. He had helped his mother in the same way when he was younger. His mother often said that he would never leave her side while she was still canning. He would stay with her no matter the day, the hour or the circumstance. The kitchen would have to be cleaned completely so that when he sat down, she could sit down too.

If there is such a thing as a godly seed, I believe that it was placed in Elias from the beginning because he was always a family man. He loved his home and family. His mother said that Elias never gave her any trouble. He was kind and gentle. The only time that she could remember him getting in trouble was in his early years. Before he was saved he decided to drink moonshine and got very drunk. He tried to slip up the steps to his room without her knowing it. But she noticed that he did not wash his feet. Every night, even as a young child, he took a bath and then washed his feet before going to sleep. Yet, this night he did not take a bath or wash his feet but slipped up to bed. When she came into his room and found out that he was drunk, she woke him up and had a long talk with him. This conversation alone was enough to make him never want to drink again. God was preparing him for the life that was before him.

Elias was a man who truly loved all children, especially his own. When we would go to Georgia on a visit, we would take the nephews and nieces fishing and hunting. If the nephews wanted the catch cooked at three or four o'clock in the morning, he would clean and cook it for them. When they all went hunting, he taught them the right way to use a shotgun. At my husband's funeral, one nephew said that Elias could have had fifty children and enjoyed every one of them.

Elias had four brothers and one sister. When his oldest brother brought Elias to my house when I was eight years old, Elias said, "I will marry that girl, Dot." He always remembered how I was dressed that day, in a blue shirt and overalls with my hair cut short. I must have made an impression on him even though he was three years older! He did not make the same impact on me because I just do not remember him at that age. Later on he got my attention so completely that I married him.

From afar, he watched me grow up. I had a blind date with him when I was older. I was in Douglas, Georgia, one Saturday when my girl-friend came up and asked whether I would go out with her and her boyfriend, who was a cousin of Elias. Knowing that the purpose was that I would date Elias, I at first said no because I didn't date anyone I didn't know. Yet, I changed my mind.

We went to a theater that night and dated a few times later. After several dates he assumed that we were going steady even though I knew nothing about it. Then suddenly he left town.

When he came back, I was not the same young woman that he left. During his absence I had met Jesus. From that time on I only dated boys who attended the Church of God. Elias had no problem with that. In fact, we became hard workers for the Lord together. We would pick up young people and carry them to church with us. Our local preacher was so impressed that he preached a sermon called "Working for the Lord" and dedicated it to both of us.

We both had a heart for our families and wanted God to use us to touch them as well. Though our fathers had similar professions, their lives were very different. My father had been married to a cherished lady named Lillie before my mother ever knew him. They had one daughter and were expecting their second child when tragedy struck. A man just released from prison murdered Lillie and her unborn child. My father and another friend had used their influence to have this man released from the chain gang. Within ten days of his release, he committed this horrific murder while my father and a farmworker were working in the field. The brutality of this murder shocked the whole community and was unheard of at this time in Georgia.

The fiendishness of the murder was so great that it disturbed and shook the whole nation. It was reported in the Associated Press and national newspapers on May 2, 1918. The *Cordelle Dispatch* reported on the murder, recording:

> Mrs. Simmons was a small woman, but she was not frail. If there was the slightest resistance to the brute attack, there was no evidence left. The dining room, stove, and a table containing the cooking things in the small cook room were in their place and not disordered. If anything was thrown to the floor in a scuffle, it had been replaced by the fiend. Only two bloody table forks were found in the yard. The bludgeon with which Mrs. Simmons head was battered to a pulp with was nowhere to be found...Further, Mrs. Simmons was attacked with forks. She was stabbed so often with the fork attack that the top of a pepper duster could not have possibly contained more perforations. The forks were both bent up in the attack so as to render them useless in a further assault of this character. This stabbing with the forks indicated that the murderer thought thus to reach her heart and end her life. But the bludgeon was apparently later used and as many as five or six terrible strokes were plainly apparent in the different apertures in her head on the right side in the temple and over the right eye. Her sewing was still under the needle of her machine on the front porch of the house. Her shoes were in the room adjoining the kitchen. She lay in her

stocking feet, her dress and underwear
partially stripped away from her neck and
right shoulder, but still pinned with two
safety pins. About her throat were slight
signs that she may have first been choked
into insensibility, and around her, the
blood from her body had flowed directly
across the room. Her brains were shat-
tered and scattered to the walls of the
kitchen by the powerful strokes of the
implement of death used by the brute...[1]

The shock of the horrifying experience of
finding his wife murdered and seeing his first
child crawling in the blood of her dead mother
left unimaginable scars on my father that just
could not be healed without divine intervention.
It is the baptism of the Holy Spirit and spiritual
gifts that release the power of God to set people
free. Remember that Psalm 55:22 says, "Cast thy
burden upon the LORD, and he shall sustain thee:
he shall never suffer the righteous to be moved."

The problem, however, was that my father
was not saved! If he had been saved, this horrifying tragedy might never have taken place. If only
he had walked in the arms of Jesus all his life,
this murder might not have seen the light of day.
If he had known Jesus he would not have had to
carry this burden until he was seventy-five years
old and finally saved. If he had only confessed
with his mouth the Lord Jesus and believed with
his heart, he would have received divine help.

After the murder and before my father

married his second wife, who became my mother, something strange and demonic took place in his life. It began very simply. He had a new horse and buggy and was traveling by a cemetery near dusk. As he approached the cemetery, he stopped to step out of the buggy and began to walk the horse for a time. While he had stopped to give his horses a rest many times before, he never stopped by a cemetery. He had been raised to fear demonic activity, instead of believing in the protection of the blood of Christ. Because of his fear, he did not go near a cemetery since it was commonly believed that demons resided there.

Everything seemed all right at the cemetery until my father saw something gray that resembled a small dog such as a poodle. There were no dogs like this where my father lived in Georgia. Instead of fleeing the cemetery and this phenomenon of the supernatural, he ran after it and tried to pick it up. I do not know how long my father continued trying to grasp this apparition. I do know that it disappeared and he could not find it again. I believe that this apparition was a demonic spirit resembling the form of a dog because after this event, my father was never the same. It was as if something had possessed him that was not holy, good or righteous. I believe that he became demon-possessed.

Why would this apparition entice my father to follow it? I believe it was for his destruction! The Scriptures warn all humanity about trafficking with demonic spirits. (See Leviticus 20:6; Deuteronomy 18:11; 1 Samuel 28:7–25; 2 Kings 21:6; 23:24; 1 Chronicles 10:13; 2 Chronicles 33:6; Isaiah 8:19; 19:3; 29:4.) My father did this in ignorance, but others do it intentionally.

My mother came into the picture about three years later. When she married my father she got a ready-made family. Not once can I remember my mother complaining about her mother-in-law or about her stepchild. It seems, from all evidence, that she loved her stepdaughter as her own. His family and the family of his first wife were always welcomed in our house. My step-grandfather was often seen around our farm. There was no contention between the families, with all trying their best to get along and make what living they could.

My mother was strong, well rounded, well meaning, determined, hard working and loved being at home. If she had not been, the marriage would have failed. In later years, my mother became so attached to her old homeplace that when my father built her a new house, her children had to go and move her out. She did not want to go, but agreed to it for the sake of her children. She centered her life around her family and her home.

There were six girls and just one boy in my family. Before World War II, and especially through the Great Depression, my father worked outside the farm and my mother hired men to help her work on the farm. It was often said that my father would work all day selling groceries, catch a train home at midnight or one A.M., and then walk about five miles with a sack filled with groceries that contained nothing but essentials. These were things that could not be grown on the farm such as salt, flour and coffee.

I am sorry to say that by the time I was born, the damaging effects of my father's past life had already taken a heavy toll on what remained of his life. He led a life of rebellion, drunkenness and debauchery. These ungodly manifestations were foreign to his upbringing and how he had lived before the tragedy hit his life. Before this time, my father had been a well-known baseball player. My father-in-law remarked that he had seen my father pitch in baseball games many times. Even though he worked in some capacity with the federal government, he still continued to work on his own farm.

He began drinking when he left the federal government and began working for the state government of Georgia. At that time he never drank anything stronger than soda. What put him on this path of destruction can be blamed in part on his participation in cocktail parties after closing. Drinking socially led him into deeper depths of sin. I believe that if he had any idea that this could have robbed him of his dignity and hurt his family, he would have never started down this path. Too many saints follow this slippery path back into sin and depravity. Paul himself warns in 1 Corinthians 6:9–10 and 1 Corinthians 9:27,

that sin is death. "For the wages of sin is death;
but the gift of God is eternal life through Jesus
Christ our Lord" (Romans 6:23). My father truly
tasted the wages of sin! Yet five years before he
died, he tasted the divine presence of the Lord
and the loving grace of God when he received the
gift of eternal life. The salvation of a soul is what
counts more than anything else does. Thank God
my father woke up before it was too late!

By the time I was six, my mother was leading
three of her children into the field to plow, plant
and break up the hard ground. Our lives
depended on it. The farm sustained us in the
worst of times. Because my mother excelled at
both cooking and farming, she could teach
anyone how to work on a farm. Countless times I
have seen her pick cotton so fast that it would
bewilder the mind. It was said that she and the
children could pick a full bale of cotton in two
days. During this time, my alcoholic father was
very little help.

Mother's cooking was legendary. Community
lore said that if anyone tasted her cooking, they
would never forget it. She never had any idea how
many would eat at our table on a given day. People
would feel her warm welcome even when they
had invited themselves. After working for some
time in the field, Mother would leave to go into the
kitchen and begin to cook lunch or dinner. When
the children came in to eat, there would always be
plenty of food. At special times there would even
be a churn of ice cream or old-fashioned teacakes.

We worked hard and also ate very well. I often remember my mother going into a cold kitchen and cooking a large breakfast with homemade biscuits, homemade butter and homemade syrup. Despite having so many wonderful memories of my mother, I would never want those days to come back!

In later years, my mother's health began to fail and that put more work on all the children, especially after my sister married. When we came home from school, it was common for us to pick a wagonload of cucumbers to take to the market. We would take the wagon down by the railroad track at night and hope that no train would come by to frighten the mule. This would make him spill the cucumbers that we wanted to sell. We had to try to keep the mule calm so that we could keep all our cucumbers. These trips to the market gave my father extra money.

Though times were hard and money not easy to come by, we were always allowed to buy what we wanted to eat when we took our goods to market. Most of the time we bought an RC Cola and cinnamon buns, charging them to my father's account. My father didn't care what we bought as long as we did not waste the money or buy things he disapproved of. We knew what to buy and what not to buy. If we bought something that my father disapproved of, we knew that we would be punished. We did have to work for the money to buy our own clothes for school and for anything else.

All of us knew what it was to dip turpentine, cut trees down for wood, sit up all night to fire a tobacco barn and crop the tobacco the next morning. There were always mules to be fed and cows to be attended to. There was never time for rest, for prayer or for God. My father was wonderful when he was not drinking and would help anyone who was less fortunate. Yet when he drank, a force would take over his life and personality. He beat us so brutally that blood would sometimes flow from our backs. He never knew when to stop. It was quite easy for him to quote, "Spare not the rod." (See Proverbs 22:15; 23:13; 29:15.)

The last time I remember my father whipping me with a tobacco stick was when he was drinking. I received this beating because I could not plow a watermelon patch planted in a dried up and rocky field. It had not rained for a considerable length of time. When he whipped me on this occasion, I refused to cry. This made him very angry and he continued to hit me harder. My mother walked outside and saw what was going on. She ran to him, took away the tobacco stick and shouted, "You are going to kill her!" Finally he stopped. I was a young teenager at that time and warned him that it was the last time that he would beat me or ever lay his hands on me again. The next day he was very sorrowful over the whole incident, especially since he himself could not plow the same piece of field.

So often I remember my father leaving the

house to go to town. I would wonder whether he was going to come back home drunk or sober. Due to his drunkenness and the horrible beatings the other children and I suffered, I often prayed to God as a child that my father would die before he came home. I prayed this as an innocent little child, not yet saved by the blood of Christ. Later, I thanked God that He knew best and did not grant my petition!

We were not a religious family, but occasionally went to church. Having no car, we had to walk. Despite our limited attendance, I saw evidence of my mother's faith frequently. She prayed and believed that it would rain before it was too late to save the crops. The rains would then come just in time. She always held to this faith and was never disappointed. Even my father was never too drunk to pray grace over his meal.

In these early years, God did not abandon my family or me. On one cold day when I was about five years of age, my overalls caught fire, and my leg was burned so badly that my parents thought I would never walk again. But a preacher was running a revival close to our house and was blessed with the power of the Holy Spirit upon his life. He came into my house and prayed for my leg. In a few days I was up and walking. God completely healed my leg.

I remember one Easter when my brother and I were walking to church. The Sunday school teacher at the church happened to be a lady who helped us put in tobacco. The next time we

worked together she remarked that if everyone
came to church all the time rather than just on
Easter or Christmas, the church would be filled.
I challenged her saying that even though she was
my Sunday school teacher, there did not seem to
be a difference between us. She smoked and
cursed like I did. She smoked publicly while I
snuck around so that my parents would not
know. This conversation led my teacher to judge
herself and accept the Lord as her Savior. I saw
such a difference in her after that. In fact, she
seemed very peculiar to me. The Scriptures say
that the saints of God are a peculiar people. (See
1 Peter 2:9.) Notice that she was teaching the
Word of God before she was saved. How many
are either teaching or preaching the Word of God
and are not saved today? Many people going to
hell are those who are present at church and
have never yet known that glorious relationship
with Christ.

In a particular Church of God, there was a
lady with whom my father had a sexual affair.
This took place a long time before she was saved
and a long time before she attended this church.
I knew about the affair and was hurt over it. I did
not like that particular Church of God because
she attended it. The affair caused untold troubles
in our family, especially to my mother.

Knowing this woman, I often swore that when
I was grown, I would beat her senseless. I always
remarked that if that church allowed women like
this to go there, I did not want any part of that

church. I did not realize that long after that affair had ended, the Lord Jesus had saved her, and she had become a new creation in Christ Jesus. There is a difference between the old you and the new you when Christ comes into your life. If not, there is no true conversion at all.

Another strike against this church was that it was Pentecostal. I was not familiar with it and had never seen what went on there. I had never experienced the shouting, the strange utterances of tongues, the healings, the miracles and the other manifestations of the Holy Spirit. The very first time I was exposed to these was a shocking experience. As it happened, I spent one night with my Aunt Hazel and my cousin. As the youngest teenager I had to sleep between them in the only bedroom. About four o'clock in the morning, I was awakened by the strange and awful commotion of my aunt jumping, shouting and speaking something strange which I had never heard in my life. I believe that my hair actually stood up. I ran behind my cousin and said, "If she gets me, she has to get you first!" When Aunt Hazel began to calm down, she lifted her hands in the air, walked into the kitchen, and all that I could hear her say was something like, "I thank the Ghost." From childhood, my family and I would sit around the fire and, on occasion, tell ghost stories. I was scared and ready to leave that place, even if I had to make a door to get out. When she walked back into the bedroom, I heard her plainly thanking the "Holy Ghost" and praising God for His visitation.

As she was thanking the Lord, I was looking around to see if I could see the Lord, too. Finally, the manifestation of the Holy Spirit subsided. My aunt said, "Kids, we can go back to bed now." I pointed my finger at my cousin and said, "This time, you sleep beside her!" Often I heard my aunt say that she wanted to leave this world shouting and speaking in tongues. God granted her desire and that is just what happened.

One night as I was attending that same Church of God, a lady preacher, Sister Mae Terry, was the guest speaker. Her sermon was not a sermon made for itching ears, nor was it a sermon filled only with empty words. (See 2 Timothy 4:3.) Her words were ones of power.

In these later years, it reminds me of a sermon preached by Jonathan Edwards. The sermon was called "Sinners in the Hands of an Angry God." When Jonathan Edwards preached this sermon, the hearers felt hell and its torments all around them. So much conviction was wrought by this sermon that hundreds would run to the altar to be saved. Jonathan Edwards would continue to preach this sermon to new hearers. This sermon never became old or outdated because it had the fire of God within it.

Just like the sermon that Jonathan Edwards preached so long ago, Sister Mae Terry preached a hell, fire and brimstone sermon. I personally believed that the seat I was sitting on was on fire when she gave the altar call. At first, all I remember was that somehow I found myself down at the altar crying out to Jesus to save my soul. The next thing I remember was a woman behind me praying with her hand upon my back. Her hand felt like a warm iron. I turned around to see just who she was and saw the woman who had the affair with my father. That night God burned away all the bitterness and hatred that I had held for years against her. I truly became that new creation in Christ Jesus that Paul speaks of in 2 Corinthians 5:17. All the baggage of my life was unpacked and put away.

As a young teenager that night, I met and fell in love with Jesus. His love was a love that I knew nothing about. Once I experienced it, I was not going to give it up, whatever the cost. As if there were not enough tears already shed, there would be much more crying in the coming years for my son and for my family. I had no idea just how much I was going to need Jesus. I could neither imagine the pain or the anguish that I would endure.

When I was saved that night, the Church of God did not take it too seriously. They saw the type of family I was born into and concluded that I would never make it. But God knew that, "He which hath begun a good work in you will perform it until the day of Jesus Christ" (Philippians 1:6). That has been proven in my life! My salvation only provided greater reinforcement to my desire to remain sexually pure until marriage. I also decided to date boys who had found the same Savior that I had.

When I was saved that night, I began a life of intercessory prayer for my family. At this time, no one in my family was saved. I was the baby girl and the only one standing in the gap for my family. Next to be saved were my older sister and brother-in-law. For years the life and practice of intercessory prayer for my family (and especially for my father) did not bear much fruit that I could see. In fact, circumstances of life became worse. My father began to drink more instead of less. When I began to intercede for my family, I entered into the battle for their very souls. It did not seem as if I was gaining much ground for a time. All I could do was trust that the Lord would lead me every step of the way. I really did not even know how to pray. I would find a place in the field and cry out to God, learning how to pray in stages. I would pray on the school bus, walking and even in my bed, crying until I went to sleep.

One particular Sunday I was in great travail over my family. After praying at the altar, I went to my Sunday school class to continue to pray. I felt such a heavy burden for my family that needed to be lifted. As I cried out to God for help, the Lord gave me a vision and told me that if I would serve Him, He would save my whole family, including my father. When the vision faded, I looked and saw my Aunt Hazel praying with me. At the time I had no idea that it would be twenty years before this vision would come true. God simply told me that my father would be saved. God gave me a piece of the puzzle, not all of the pieces at once. It might have seemed easier for God to give it all to me at once. But where would my faith have been?

During these twenty years my father's condition did not get any better but actually became worse. Later there would only be a few days that he would not be drinking. But even these days were terrible because he would suffer withdrawal symptoms. During these times it was very common for him to have hallucinations of elephants, pink rats running up the wall and other images. My mother finally gave up and put him in a hospital where he could receive help for his alcoholism. He was not ready to receive the help and became angrier than ever. When he finally left the hospital, he went back to the same type of life that he had before.

After this failed treatment I had to take my parents to the tobacco market one Saturday. I could tell that my father had been drinking that morning just like he did most days. I did not let on that I knew he had been drinking whiskey. I asked, "Dad, you have been good today. I know that you want a drink. Where do you buy your whiskey? It is time that this family acknowledges that we have an alcoholic father rather than being ashamed of it anymore." I gave him twenty dollars and took him to the liquor store. When he came out I said to him, "Is that enough to last till Monday?" I did not want him driving on the road in a drunken state. His remark to me was, "Now, let's not overdo this thing!" I said to him, "We have tried to get help for you to quit drinking with no success. The god that you serve is the god of alcoholism. When you die, I am going to put a fifth of whiskey in your coffin, because that fifth of whiskey is the god that is sending you to hell for all eternity!" My father was ready to receive help the following Monday morning. This time the hospital made it hard on him. The medical staff put him in with mental patients that had severe problems. My father was frightened for his very life. He prayed that if God would let him live, he would serve Him and never drink again. At that moment, my father was saved. His last testimony before his death was, "Since I have found the Master, I have found no detour signs." This same message was preached at my father's funeral.

Even though my father was saved, God was not finished with our family and had not yet fulfilled His entire promise to me. One by one, my family began to come into the fullness of the Lord. I have found that God always brings to pass what He promises, as long as we do our part. The last unsaved person in my family came to know the Lord only two years before the writing of this book.

Chapter Two

BATTLE FOR A MIRACLE

The spiritual warfare for my family began long before the battle for my son. The fight to receive a miracle for my son really began before I was married. The Lord was preparing me and warning me that there would be an assault ahead.

Elias and I prayed earnestly for a year about the decision to marry. In 1951, we tied the knot and soon afterward moved down to Jacksonville, Florida. We made this unheard of move away from everything that we knew, even though we had no money and a small job that paid very little. Unaware that God was moving us out of our safety zone, we found ourselves in Jacksonville in miserable conditions. For two years we barely survived. Cabbage and grits became our mainstay because they were cheap. It is amazing to me that even now I still enjoy eating them. After God saw that He could trust us with the little we had, He gave us better jobs and helped us save some money.

Before that, I relentlessly prayed that God would give me a good job even though it did not seem likely. I told Him that I would never use it selfishly. Elias and I continued to attend church even though we were looked down upon because we had such poor clothes. Elias even walked to work to save gas so that we could go to church. One night we decided to go to a church near our home. The preacher saw that I had no stockings on and preached against me not wearing them.

Easter was coming up and I realized that I would have to wear the same old dress that I had been wearing during the week. Finally, the Lord blessed me with a very good job. I began to put money back, dollar by dollar, to buy an expensive Easter outfit. I was able to save one hundred and fifty dollars, a huge sum to me at the time.

I had planned my shopping trip for the Saturday before Easter. I was so excited about getting a new dress! The Lord, however, had not forgotten my promise to Him that I would be unselfish with my earnings once I got my new job. The Wednesday before Easter, the Lord led me to a particular home. There I found an elderly woman and her disabled son. They were both very sick and had been to the doctor. They had no money to buy medicine or food. Their kitchen cabinets were bare and they had no gas to cook with.

I took their prescriptions to a pharmacy and ran into the grocery store. I decided to spend enough money to buy a little food for them, so that they could survive for a few days. As I was walking down the aisles, I will never forget what the Lord said to me.

The simple words I heard were, "Feed them as you want Me to feed you." I pushed down hard on the brakes of that cart. I decided to buy for them more than I would have bought for myself. When I checked out, I had spent all of the money that I had saved. I rose Easter Sunday and got ready to go to church. Since I had spent my money, I had to wear a dress that was made of a heavy material and not really suitable for the Easter season. Evangelist T. L. Lowery was having a baptismal service in a tent. When I arrived, I decided to sit in the very back, hoping that no one would see me. But the Lord had other plans in mind! Our pastor and his wife had saved seats for us right down front. As I sat down, I felt led to pray that I would be able to shout for joy, just as my Aunt Hazel once did.

The baptismal service seemed dead. In an instant of time though, the Holy Spirit began to move in our midst in a mighty way. All at once, I jumped up, ran down the aisle across the platform, and jumped into the baptismal pool shouting from one end to the other. The ushers could not pull me out of the pool. Our pastor said, "If that water is holy enough to make Dot Roberts shout, let us all go into it." There were several hundred baptized that day. I was the first one in and the last one out. My heavy dress went right into the water with me and did not come up over my head. God's plan was working all along.

In the tenth year of a childless marriage, the Lord led me to begin praying for a child. I remembered the prayers of the childless in the Bible and how God answered them. God put a seed of faith in my heart that led me to pray not just for a child, but also for a son. After praying for some time, the Lord told me to name my boy Ricky Elias Roberts. When my husband came home from work that night, I told him that we would have a son and what we were to name him. My husband was upset because he knew that my doctors had advised me not to have children due to medical reasons. I told him, "We are going to have faith to believe that God can bring me through this, or we can just hang up on this thing called faith. We are either going to believe or reject God's promise." I was fired-up and meant business. I was determined to push forward to receive what God had for me. Often we don't receive the things that God has for us because we won't push forward.

Nine months later our son was born. Even before the birth, our peace and rest disappeared. The pregnancy was not easy and I began to have all kinds of complications. Everything imaginable that could happen did happen in our lives. Satan literally came upon us like a flood. Satan is such a coward because he catches us at our weakest times and then turns all his forces loose against us.

Even in the midst of all the tribulation, God would use us to pray for people who were sick, and they would recover. This was especially true after my son was born. I felt as if I was experiencing the full gospel of the apostolic church. I saw God performing miracles and healings before my very eyes. I saw the words of Christ being fulfilled right in front of me, "They shall lay hands on the sick, and they shall recover" (Mark 16:18). I remembered the words of James also coming to pass, "And the prayer of faith shall save the sick, and the Lord shall raise him up; and if he have committed sins, they shall be forgiven him" (James 5:15).

During this time, Satan often put someone who was either fanatical or demon-possessed in my path. I remember meeting a recently saved woman who fanatically prophesied many crazy things. I began to fast up to twelve days at a time because I did not know how to handle this woman's situation and hysteria, nor did I know how to handle the spirit of deception that had fallen upon her. She actually believed that she was the reincarnation of a famous prophet. Finally, she prophesied that if Elias and her husband would go to a certain place, they would find a man that would be able to help her. There was no such man because he did not exist! She came to the realization that her prophecies were not of God and that she had been deceived. She repented of her sins and became spiritually balanced by following 1 John 5:5–10.

All of these experiences burdened me so much that I backed off from God and stayed in my safety zone for some time. In this lukewarm state, I found out that Satan left me alone because I was not challenging him. I found out that staying in the safety zone just doesn't work. Just as the mother eagle pushes her babies out of the nest, so the saint of God will have battles to go through to gain God's promise. As long as I remained in my comfort zone, Satan was winning the battle for my son because I was no threat to him. God challenged me to leave that place of security and I accepted. I was now ready to do battle for my family and son. I was ready to do spiritual warfare. I was ready to go through dark places. I was ready to seek after God and His presence more completely than I had ever done before. Whatever I had to fight, whatever battle I had to go through, I was ready. I decided that no matter what opposition I encountered, I was going to hang on to the altar of God until I touched the hem of Jesus' garment. No matter what it took, I was going to touch that robe for my son. The Bible proclaims, "By whose stripes ye were healed" (1 Peter 2:24).

I thank God that I had first-hand experience with the retarded even before my son was born. My oldest sister, Myrtle, was born severely retarded. I knew the heartache that filled our whole family and the helplessness that we felt. Her retardation was due to a birth defect. The distress of my mother over her retarded daughter and the drunkenness of my father were so great, that it is hard to imagine how she survived. My sister lived to be forty-nine, nine years longer than the doctors had predicted.

When Ricky was born, the doctors advised me

that I would never raise him because he was too sickly. I said, "Yes, but the Lord God gave him to Elias and me. We will raise him." During the first six years of his life, we slept with an alarm clock going off every thirty minutes. One minute, Ricky would be all right and the next minute we would be on our way to the emergency room. We did not realize that our child was mentally disabled or retarded. He had severe brain damage and dyslexia. We did not know that, even with his disability, Satan would turn against him even more, throwing fiery darts of sickness upon him.

In particular, Ricky would endure terrible fevers and convulsions. It seemed that he suffered from sickness all the time. If he became excited or stressed-out, his sickness would become worse. Since he could be sick at any moment, we could not let him play like other children. It seemed as if little changes in our lives, like the weather or a cold, would bring on sickness. When his fever went above one hundred and one degrees, convulsions would also be present. Ricky could change from being physically well to being physically ill within seconds. From moment to moment, Elias and I never knew what would happen. We did not know whether we would have a normal day or spend all day and night at the hospital.

Satan again struck my son in a way that I never anticipated. One day Ricky woke up and was paralyzed, unable to walk. Our doctor examined him and said that there was nothing that could help. We fell upon our knees and cried out to God. At the end of three months Ricky experienced God's healing power and was able to walk. He was able to take small steps and then larger ones. Finally, within days, all the negative effects that he had suffered from that attack were gone. He could walk normally.

It was in the midst of crying over my son that I called my son's pediatrician, Dr. Frame, and asked him if I could come to the office to talk to him about Ricky. I was crying hysterically when I got to his office, feeling that I was a bad mother since my son could not stay well. The doctor was very kind and had a long talk with me. He suggested that Elias and I put down carpet all over the house so that our son would not be on the cold tile floors. We did that, but it did not seem to help. Ricky still had colds and sinus infections and suffered constantly with tonsillitis, bronchitis, ear inflammation and many other things. The first six years of his life seemed a constant battle against illness.

We had been to the hospital so many times that the nurses knew who we were and were ready for us when we came in. All that we knew to do was to stand and pray as Daniel did in Daniel 9. We had no idea about what was happening to us or why these calamities seemed to descend upon our small family. We were at the end of our hope, and our faith was stretched to its very limit. We had gone as far as we could physically go. When we reach this breaking point,

God always steps into the picture.

Within the first six years of Ricky's life, God stepped into the picture in a particular and special manner. He sent an evangelist to Jacksonville when my son was about four years old who prayed that Ricky would sleep and be able to overcome his insomnia. We were used to Ricky sleeping for thirty minutes and being awake for eight hours or more. The only time that Elias and I were able to sleep soundly and without worry during these times was when my mother-in-law would come down and take care of Ricky. She was a wonderful praying saint of God who prayed constantly for our son and his deliverance. Many more joined her in praying for a miracle for Ricky.

We began to realize that apart from God, we could do little to help Ricky. This sense of helplessness brought us to our knees. God led me into a season of intense intercession. To obey I had to be willing to eliminate everything that distracted me from perfect obedience.

As I was cooking supper one day, Ricky had a convulsion and fell out of his high chair onto our tile floor. I did not move him until my neighbor came and checked to see if any bones had been broken. Another time, I was tied up in traffic, and Ricky had a bad convulsion. All I could do was put my finger in his mouth to keep him from chewing his tongue until I could get him to a hospital. Elias and I never had any warning about his convulsions. Most of the time I was not alone when this happened. This was another evidence of God's mercy.

I remember the night he was going to graduate from kindergarten. Ricky had a double convulsion, and his face turned black. I thought I was going to lose him! Thank God for the doctor and the nurse that were there that night. Despite their skill, we all felt truly helpless. Medically, they could only treat the symptoms, but through prayer and the laying on of hands, God could heal him totally. He never had another seizure after that night.

As I look back, I realize that the wisest decision Elias and I ever made was to become Christians. I thought as a teenager that I needed Jesus, but I did not realize that I was going to need Him even more for my son. Elias and I began to understand that we had to have more help, and that it had to come from God alone!

As Ricky continued to grow up physically, both Elias and I began to grow more serious about our relationship with Jesus. Everything that the world had to offer meant nothing to us. The significance of material things began fading into the shadows before the intense sorrow over our son. Even though I loved coaching my softball team, I gave it up to study the Word of God and stay in my prayer closet for my son.

Elias and I began to realize that our son was truly retarded when he entered kindergarten. It did not take us long to find out that he could not distinguish one letter from another. We became frantic that Ricky did not know the difference between letters. The kindergarten teacher tried to calm our concerns by pointing out that he was just a young five-year-old. I was to hear repeatedly, "Don't worry! He is just not old enough yet to learn." When Ricky began elementary school, the same statement was made in both the first and second grades. The teachers gave excuse after excuse about why Ricky could not learn. They accused him of suffering from excitability, anxiety and hyperactivity. None of these accusations were true. They did not have time to worry about one child among countless others in the classroom. One child falling through the cracks of the school system did not warrant their attention.

No matter what my husband and I did to help Ricky learn, it was unsuccessful. Yet, we continued to try. All through the second, third and fourth grades, we continued to try and teach the alphabet one letter at a time. We would write phrases on cards like, "Ricky and Snoopy" (his dog). As long as the cards were up, Ricky could repeat with us what was written on them. However, he could not pronounce any of the words or remember the phrases when the cards were taken down, hidden or covered. He would then begin to cry anew.

The next few years were no better. The school system and the teachers kept saying that Ricky had no learning problems. They passed him from grade to grade even though he could not read a simple word. One of my neighbors, Virginia

Harrell, who was a substitute teacher, saw first-hand how the teachers treated my child. They did not encourage him to do anything. They would not even make him stand up for the pledge of allegiance. They gave up on him. But, thank God, we did not! But what is even more important is that God never gave up on Ricky!

Ricky was just sitting in the classroom, taking up space. The teachers did not know what to do when I would go to talk to any of them. I even asked the school to have him tested repeatedly. The absence of concern on the part of the school system exasperated me. I felt that they had turned their back on my child. Because I was so concerned about my son, I made an appointment with the guidance clinic through the school board. The specialists kept Ricky for about three hours testing him. They called me with good news. Though he could not read a word or a letter, they concluded that he was mentally normal. They implied that I was too overprotective. They wanted to punish him for not learning. This I would not allow.

While I am not a doctor or psychologist, I believe that the spirit of my son knew that something was wrong with his brain. He seemed to intuitively understand that he was not like other children. We would catch him sitting and crying by himself many times. Ricky even resorted to paying other children to play games with him.

I decided that I needed to do whatever I had to do, to get help for Ricky. We hired tutors and placed our son in a learning institution that dealt with children who have learning difficulties. One of these institutions was known as Reading Researcher Institution and was headed by Dr. Skinner. We still have the canceled checks proving that Ricky did enter this institution.

Ricky attended another institution that has long since ceased its operation. One day he tried to run away, slamming into a glass door so hard that it almost broke. The teachers there were constantly yelling, and Ricky couldn't take it any more. After this, Ricky came very close to having a nervous breakdown. His father found him shaking uncontrollably while trying to crawl under a car. Elias picked him up, wrapped his arms around him, and said, "Ricky, whether you ever learn or not, your mother and I love you. We will work and save for you." When they came through the door, I turned off dinner, took him in my arms, and said the same thing that Elias had said. We all cried together.

I finally sought help through the pediatrician who had worked with us for so long in dealing with Ricky's problems. I told him my fears and my belief that Ricky suffered from a form of learning disability known as dyslexia. He informed me that he believed that his son also had dyslexia. He shared that he had sent his son to a leading specialist in Gainesville. He sent us there.

The doctor and his staff spent three days testing and analyzing Ricky. At our consultation, the doctor called us in to tell us that Ricky not only had dyslexia, but severe brain damage as well. There was nothing more that he could do medically. Ricky, according to this specialist, could never learn anything. In addition to his three close calls with a nervous breakdown, his IQ was extremely low. He would never be able to live anything close to a normal life. As he said this, the Holy Spirit rose up within me and prayed, "No! He won't! For as long as Jesus Christ sits at the right hand of the Father, my son will never go through life like that. I asked God for the gift of a son, and my Father knows how to give only good gifts to his people."

The specialist stayed with us for four hours, teaching us ways to deal with Ricky. We were unaware that Ricky was outside the room listening to all of this. Can you imagine what he must have felt upon hearing that nothing could ever be done for him?

Leaving Gainesville to come home was the loneliest time that Elias and I ever spent. We had hit rock bottom. During the trip back home I sat very quietly with my arms around Ricky and spoke few words. When we finally arrived home, we made a covenant with the Lord. We gave the Lord everything we had. We cleaned out our bank account and gave it all to God. We dedicated our son to God, acknowledging that we did not have the ability to raise him in our own strength. In essence, we gave God our whole lives and began living a new life with God at the core. Both Elias and I began a life of fasting and prayer, seeking God to be over our child and over our lives.

It was during this intense fire of suffering that we experienced God's purifying power working in all of us. Until that point in our lives, I can truthfully say that I had never been completely sold-out to God. I paid the preacher to read the Bible, understand its mysteries, and do the praying for the congregation and for the nation. God showed us how false this way of thinking is. God has called each of us to get into His Word and apply it for ourselves. We can't depend on someone to do it for us.

Elias and I began to study the Bible, researching it and studying church history and theology. We began to teach Ricky what the Bible said about faith, prayer and healing. As we put him to bed at night, I would read the Bible and pray with him. I would tell him that God loved him and wanted to heal him. I would quote Scriptures on healing from the books of Isaiah and James.

We did not know at the time that Ricky was praying as well. After Elias and I would return to our room, Ricky would cover his head and pray that God would heal him and make him like other children. Ricky frequently asked, "Lord, why can't I be healed and be like other children?" When we found his pillow wet with tears, he admitted that he also had been crying aloud to God for his healing. It was so heartbreaking to see our son crying out to God with so much anguish and pain. He was retarded, yet his spirit knew what was going on and how hurt he felt by the children who taunted him. Ricky did not realize that he had entered into a life of prayer where patience is practiced, learned and understood.

Ricky continued to pray, just as his father and I did. Our faith and our prayer life were all that we had. During those painful years, I prayed day and night, weeping before the Lord God for my son. Though I did not consciously understand intercessory prayer, I was practicing it.

In 1973, Ricky still attended public school. He continued to be passed from one grade to another, until as a sixth grader he could not spell or write his name. At this time, Virginia Harrell again came to our rescue. She knew that the public school that Ricky attended was doing nothing for him. One evening she came to our house to tell us that University Christian School had a special education class with only ten pupils. She thought this would be a good place for Ricky since the teacher was trained to help disabled children.

The morning that I took Ricky to register was a very bad day. He pitched a fit about leaving the public school for University Christian. I would drive a few miles, pull over and offer to carry Ricky back to the other school. I made it clear that he had to go to school somewhere. At last, I pulled the car off the road and sat and cried. When Ricky saw how painful all this was for me, he agreed to go to the new school.

When Ricky was tested, the teachers found out that, although he was twelve years old, he was mentally below a kindergarten level. Even though his academic level was too low, God made an opening for him in that class. As he began attending, the school helped all it could. However, there seemed to be very little that anyone could do for him. I still took him to tutors weekly. In the summer I began again trying to teach him at least one hundred words. Elias and I increased our prayers for him and took him to every preacher who believed in healing by prayer and the laying on of hands.

Ricky's frustration level seemed to ease at this school. He cried less and even enjoyed the bus ride to school. Ricky continued to be teased and laughed at by other children because of his disability. He was called many names that made fun of him, even though the school included the special education children in everything. For example, at Christmas the school had made a place in the Christmas program for all the kids. That night was so special for all the parents to see their children having a good time. Ricky played the prophet Isaiah in this Christmas program, foretelling the coming of the Messiah.

From 1973 to the fall of 1977, Ricky saw little success in learning. Within this time period he did advance slowly to a third grade level. No further advancement or improvement was predicted for Ricky. He seemed to have reached the highest level he could attain. We three

Chapter Three

Cost of a Miracle

During this time Satan struck against us from other directions with other storms. Our lives became complicated as Satan and his forces sought our destruction. More than ever, it became apparent that the goal of these tribulations was to prevent us from effectively battling for our son. Their purpose was to tie us down, weaken us and turn our attention away from the miracle that waited.

The first of these storms came against my sister Myrtle who lived in Douglas, Georgia. She was having surgery for intestinal cancer and was not expected to live. My family called to ask if I could come and help them. I had been through a bad car wreck and my doctor would not allow me to drive. The Lord provided a friend who drove me to see Myrtle and her family for a week. I felt like a yo-yo being pulled in many directions at the same time. The situation with Ricky, my sister in the hospital, Elias, my job and other things all combined simultaneously to tear me apart.

When I went to Augusta and found the weakened condition of my sister, I cried. In addition to her cancer surgery she had also had a colostomy redone. This second surgery made things worse instead of better. She was hanging between death and life. My other sister Ruby came to be with me, and we were so upset by the suffering our sister went through. She had such a high fever that she lay on a sheet of ice. She stayed frozen to the bed with her internal temperature constantly monitored. Ruby would take the day shift while I would take the night shift. We also hired a private nurse around the clock to help us. But our sister knew when we were in the room. If we left, her blood pressure shot up. Though she was out of it and mentally disabled, her spirit knew we were present and our hands were always upon her.

One night she was so out of it because of her high fever, I sat on the bed with my hand on her until the early morning. She began to pray the most beautiful prayer of repentance that I have ever heard in my life. She spoke words that were not in her limited vocabulary. I knew that the Holy Spirit was guiding her spirit to pray this prayer. God was allowing me to witness this awesome experience and was giving me the assurance that she was saved. Immediately, I remembered the promise that Jesus had made to me that He would save my family. The tears began to flow down my cheeks! I could not hold it in any longer as the realization of the fulfillment of God's Word hit me. Soon after Christmas, Myrtle died. I was at peace knowing that her spirit was in the hands of the Lord and that one day I would see her in Heaven, gloriously perfect.

My mother was the next person in my family that Satan attacked. She had gone to see one of my sisters and while there, a blood vessel burst in her stomach. My sister called and asked me to come and help her. We put her in the hospital even though she had no insurance. We agreed to be responsible for her bill and were worried about paying for it. The Lord provided us with a doctor that gave us a discount for both the hospital and his cost.

Some families seem to have someone who is considered the "black sheep" of the family. They go their own way and make their own rules. My sister Sue fit that description in our family. She appeared to be more like my father than the rest of his children. She was stubborn, prideful, rebellious and demanding. She loved material things and all that the world offered. My sister loved the party life, drinking, dancing and committing all sorts of evil affairs.

This was her attitude and way of thinking until she became so depraved that she destroyed herself and her family. Sue thought herself unable to give up the world and tried to find some type of Christianity that would fit her lifestyle and satisfy her soul. She tried the Jehovah Witnesses and accepted that life for a while because they taught against the doctrine of hell. Gradually she began to see that there was a real hell, not just a hell upon this earth. She saw the reality of the supernatural when she allowed a witch to live in her home. She saw firsthand the power of Satan as the witch cast spells and did incantations.

I remember that when her daughter was about three, Sue and her husband went to dinner in a restaurant with her. The waiter asked the daughter, "What would you like?" The daughter replied, "A beer." Both Sue and her husband thought it was funny. However, it was not funny at all when their daughter grew up. The seeds of destruction had been planted within their child, and she became extremely rebellious. She took countless kinds of drugs, drank excessively and led a promiscuous and reckless life. Sue's family lost everything that they had spent a lifetime working for. They had experienced financial blessing and bought all that they could buy. Only happiness eluded them. By the time she accepted the Lord, it was too late for God to give her back what Satan had stolen.

One evening the Spirit of the Lord came upon me to pray for Sue and her family after they left my home to return to theirs. "Likewise the Spirit also helps in our weaknesses. For we do not know what we should pray for as we ought, but the Spirit Himself makes intercession for us with groanings which cannot be uttered. Now He who searches the hearts knows what the mind of the Spirit is, because He makes intercession for the saints according to the will of God" (Romans 8: 26–27, NKJV).

After two hours, I called their home and shared with them that the Lord had directed me

While in my home, the demons within her began to manifest themselves right before me as her voice and her face changed. I will never forget their evil voices. The words that came out of her mouth were not her words but Satan's. I had allowed her to be in our home because I knew that the Lord would protect us. The Lord revealed to me that she wanted to kill herself. I lay on the floor in front of her bedroom door so that she could not leave to get a knife or other weapon with which to harm herself. I did not realize that she had sleeping pills with her. But God only allowed her to put the pills up to her mouth before she froze. She could not actually put them in her mouth because of God's intervention.

After that long night, I got up to fix her a good breakfast. When I came back from putting gas in the car, she had the worst look on her face. She had been notified that her husband had died, and she was in shock. I went back to her house to stay with her during his funeral. Having to leave my home and stay with my sister during this time was an experience that I will never forget. There was no place, I believe, more demonic than this home. The demons of hell could literally be heard, yelling, howling and screaming. I could hear the gnashing of teeth. The evil whispering that these spirits spoke so penetrated the atmosphere of that home, that I could only stay there by pleading the blood of Jesus over me. While my other sisters took sleeping pills to fall asleep, I remained vigilant. I felt that it was not a time for sleep but for battle. I learned firsthand about the power of the blood over every other weapon of our spiritual warfare.

The Lord became so close to me during this time. He would reveal to Elias and me things that were going to happen to our family. One night the Lord showed me that there would be an attempted shooting of my sister Sue at noon the next day. Immediately, I began to pray. But this time I prayed more powerfully than I have ever done. As I was praying, Satan spoke to me and said, "She will die tomorrow!" I told Satan, "No! As God liveth, she will not die!" I claimed her for the kingdom of God and pled the blood of Jesus over her repeatedly.

The day of my sister's attempted shooting was a terrible day. Shortly after noon, my extension at work rang with an emergency telephone call. Sue had been shot at six times but was never hit. I decided that she was not going to go to hell if I could help it. I decided to pray and fast until God moved somehow and saved her. Having no theology to discredit what God could do or what He had spoken to me, I believed in the promise God made to me. I held on to it with a death grip.

Sue suffered many debilitating problems, physical, mental and spiritual. After her husband died, the doctor found a spur growing on her spinal cord. The pain was so great that she became more dependent on drugs and alcohol. This was the only time that she experienced relief from the pain. Despite this, she tried her best to keep the business going and deal with her daughter the best way she knew how.

Her daughter married and this positively affected her behavior. She was a great wife to her husband. She would have his breakfast fixed even if she had to get up at four o'clock in the morning. She had his clothes washed and ironed. After she had their child, her husband left her. From that point on, she fell deeper and deeper into the arms of Satan and his kind of life, indulging in all kinds of sin and becoming violent. She married someone else and became pregnant with his child.

There were times when my niece was so intoxicated or on drugs that she would try to kill her husband, her mother, myself or anyone else. She stabbed her second husband, and when he was recovering in the hospital, she pulled the tubes out of him. People literally became terrified of her.

With all of these problems, my sister never took any blame for how her daughter had turned out. I wish that my sister could have lived long enough to see her daughter change, becoming a loving person and marrying a man that loved her.

One of the last times I talked to Sue and her daughter, Sue said, "I was not a good mother, but I am a wonderful grandmother." She no longer wanted to live the kind of life that sowed so many seeds of destruction. In the last years of her life, paralyzed and suffering from a stroke, she wanted Jesus. She called out to Jesus for mercy.

The Lord Himself heard her cries and in a vision came down to her. She saw Him in this vision, walking into her room and telling her how long she had to live. That night she accepted the Lord. The hatred, bitterness and stubbornness melted away and what was left behind was a sweet and loving person who loved Jesus. What I saw God doing before my eyes took forty long years of fasting and prayer to be accomplished. God kept His Word, but I did my part! From that night on she continued to say, "He's real! He's real! He's real!" Jesus became the beginning, the middle and the end of her speech. She ate, lived and slept the Word of God. She was never the same again, and God continued to keep His Word about my family.

Sue was finally put into a nursing home where I could go see about her without worrying about running into her daughter who always picked a fight. She only weighed sixty pounds. After working all day and driving about sixty miles to my job, I would run home, cook dinner and drive the same distance to feed her. It took about two hours to feed her, one bite at a time. Soon after moving into the nursing home, she died and met the Master she so longed to see.

Next, the Lord began to deal with Elias about his younger brother, Wallace, a deputy sheriff in Coffee County, Georgia. God gave Elias a vision that his brother was going to be shot with his own gun within six months. He told a pastor about what God had shown him and sought immediate prayer for his brother. The pastor anointed a that he saw the very hand of God come down from Heaven, hit his chest while the nurse screamed out loud, "I have a pulse!" All the damage caused by the bullet was instantaneously healed. Instead of weeks of recuperation, he needed none. That is just like God!

I would like to tell you that his life changed because of that experience, but it didn't happen. God gave him chance after chance, and he rebuffed them all. For the sake of Elias, God spared Wallace, but instead of changing, he fell deeper and deeper into sin. Does not the Bible say that the wages of sin are death? Twenty years later, he committed suicide with the same kind of gun with which he was shot the first time and in the same place. What a tragedy!

Another turning point in my life and the lives of my family was the death of my sister Ruby. When I heard about her death, I cried bitter tears to God. I wondered why God allowed her to die because I needed her so badly. Ruby had always been the one constant in our family, helping anyone who needed her. She had been of great help to our mother. Since I lived in Jacksonville and could only go up to Georgia occasionally, she stayed near my mother and took care of her.

Before her death, one of the greatest events in her life was the baptism of the Holy Spirit with speaking in tongues. She had always wondered about speaking in tongues, questioning whether they were biblical and whether they were for this day. All of this came to a head one day when my sister and I were in the field picking butter beans. The Lord showed me a vision that someone in our family would die. Right there I began to cry out to God for help and mercy and began to speak in tongues. Ruby was shocked, awed and worried. She had never heard anything like that. She could say nothing but, "Baby, please get a hold of yourself! You are going to have a nervous breakdown!" I said, "Sis, can't you understand what this family is about to go through? We need to get a hold of God!"

After I left her house, she fell upon her knees and cried out to God saying, "God, if speaking in tongues is real, I want it!" Then, the power of the Holy Spirit came over her and she began to speak the words of a language that she didn't know. She had never expected so much joy and peace, unknown to her and unexplainable! She received this gift three years before she died and never wanted to lose it.

After this, we were able to pray together in a completeness and power that both of us had never experienced before. Although I had experienced the baptism of the Holy Spirit years before she received it, I had not experienced this level of holiness and power. According to Deuteronomy 32:30, two can put to flight at least ten thousand. This was the first time in our family that two Spirit-filled saints were joined in the battle against the forces of evil for our family. There was another sister who was Spirit-filled, but she lived far away from the family and could not always join in the struggle.

While Ruby and I were winning the battle for our family against Satan, God warned me that Satan desired the life of my sister Ruby. I stayed on my knees and prayed using the passage about Hezekiah seeking God for mercy and protection. (See 2 Kings 20:1.) God graciously moved and her life was extended for a considerable time.

Nonetheless, there are times when no one can stand up for you in spiritual warfare, you must fight alone. While my sister Ruby was Spirit-filled, she did not know or comprehend that she was in danger and needed to fight against the wiles of Satan. I warned her that she was under direct attack by witchcraft. But she would not listen. When God warns us and we don't listen, the results can be terrible and disastrous. I believe that she succumbed to the plans of Satan and died before her time. God allowed it even though it wasn't his original intention.

My son explains the fulfillment of God's Word and His intentions in connection to free will in this way:

> The fulfillment of God's Word and God's intention is not placed outside the sphere of human freedom and choice, and most often is dependent upon free moral agents to become fulfilled. It is grace that demands that the intentions of God must allow free moral agents a choice to accept or reject God's will for their lives. When God uses a choice done by free-will

agents, He works to turn the actions of men and other creatures into a method or means by which His plans may be fulfilled. In other words, He takes those actions that are contrary to His will and takes hold of the consequences and changes things so that they may be beneficial to the fulfillment of His plans.

The day I learned that my sister Ruby had died, I lost it. I went into shock. I could not believe that God would do this to me. I cried out loudly and bitterly while walking throughout the house, yelling, "God, what are You doing to me? Do You love me? Didn't You know that the family needed her? Why have You forsaken me?" I felt that I needed her so badly to go with me through our family troubles and to give me courage. We were such a comfort to each other and could cry on one another's shoulders. She was the very heart of our family. That night I walked in the backyard asking God why. It seemed that God was a thousand miles away and had turned His face from me. It is such an awful feeling to feel that God has forsaken you! My life, which was already shaken, became worse and the storms of life seemed to rage around me more heavily.

Elias did not say anything about the death of Ruby until we were on our way to the funeral. I still could not say anything except, "Why, God, why?" Elias was the one that God enlightened and gave the reasons for her death. Elias simply said that God did not tell me about her death because I would have prayed and fasted until He would have spared her again. It was not my time to do this, but it was time for Ruby to step up and heed the warnings of the Lord. In addition, he said that my mother was another reason that God allowed this. God would work through this to save her.

In the midst of Ruby's funeral preparations, I was wondering what my family and I were going to do about Mother. Mother had burned herself very badly three days before Ruby died. I had told Ruby then that Mother was unable to live by herself due to her age and health. The day of Ruby's funeral, my family and I had to put Mother in the hospital for a skin graft on her arm. This was a terrible time. Ruby's death and my mother's accident had upset me so much. Then I found out that my mother had cancer of the liver and would not live long. I went to my car and began to cry out to God saying, "Lord, You promised me that You will not let more be put on me than I can bear" (1 Corinthians 10:13). Immediately, the Lord spoke to me saying, "Go on a five-day fast." I began to fast and a few of the nurses joined me. Three days after I completed the five-day fast, the doctor came into her room and said that he wanted to send her to another hospital for a CAT scan. At that time not all hospitals had this equipment. From Thursday through Saturday morning, the hospital ran tests. Finally, the doctor came into the room a little disturbed and bewildered. He simply said, "I do not know what to tell you about your mother. Other doctors and I have consulted together about the diagnosis and have come to the conclusion that your mother had liver cancer, but now her liver is as normal as yours and mine. I don't know what happened." I said, "Doctor, do you believe in fasting and praying?" He said, "Yes!" I said, "Doctor, God put me on a fast for this healing!" He told me to take her home.

This was the beginning of nine years of what can only be called "hell." It was overwhelming because I was still dealing with a retarded son and a mother who seemed truly demon-possessed. My mother was the hardest person to take care of that anyone had ever seen. I entered into a time of intercessory prayer more intense than any I had ever experienced.

After my sister Ruby's death, I had a vision in which the Lord carried me away into hell. I fell down deeper and deeper into a deep pit. This falling lasted for a considerable length of time. When I arrived in hell, there was darkness everywhere; yet, there was a light in the midst of that darkness. I assumed that the light must have been the light of God shining even in hell itself. It must have been the Shekinah Glory, the divine presence of the Lord being manifested. This light penetrated far enough for me to see what was going on. Though I did not literally see the dead, I saw the shadows or forms of many in hell. I saw the shapes of some that I knew did not live a holy life and were already dead. God was telling me that they had gone to hell. I saw the forms of people who were still living. I knew God was telling me that they were destined for hell if they did not change. One of these was my mother. I saw her form hanging and looking over hell. I felt that this meant that she would go to hell if she did not change. When I saw her form, I cried out to God, "Don't let her go to hell! Her life has been so hard!"

After this vision, I ran into the living room and told my husband what had happened. He said that my mother was not saved. The whole purpose of the vision was to warn me that my mother did not yet belong to God. She had lived as a hypocrite for many years, going to church though she was not saved. She knew about Jesus, but had never met Him. My dilemma was how to get my mother to realize that she was not saved.

Three weeks later, a tent revival came to Jacksonville. All of us, including my mother, went. The preacher, whom we had never seen before, said to me, "I am going to eat breakfast with you in the morning." He later told Elias that my mother had to repent of her sins, especially sins that she believed God would never forgive. He came to our home and talked to her personally and privately. While she was still not saved, this was the beginning of her deliverance. As in the early church, some are delivered from demon possession in stages. I think that this was a clear example of this. The early church said that until one is completely delivered from demonic possession, that person could not be saved.

I wish I could say that the preacher's talk to her was all that it took for her to have peace and be saved, but Satan did not want to give her up. A major battle was still going on. Elias and I had to live in intercessory prayer, learning even more deeply how to pray more fervently. Intercessory prayer became not only a ministry, but also a way of life. We learned that it can be a vehicle to really touch the heart of God. It will open doors that nothing else can open; it will bring down strongholds when nothing else can break them; it will help win the battle for our souls. Intercessory prayer, equipped with the baptism of the Holy Spirit and the evidence of speaking in tongues, will empower the saint of God like nothing else. Intercessory prayer and tears are interwoven. Tears touch God when nothing else can because they are linked to intense prayer.

Elias, Ricky and I finally found out what was troubling Mother. First, we saw three demons come out of her, each looking like a black cat. Another night we heard a horrible scream come from her room. My son and I ran into her room as she was screaming, "Get those babies off me and my bed!"

I wondered what had happened in her life to torment her so. In addition to being retarded, my sister Myrtle was not able to walk early in her life, and everything that she ate had to be cooked for three hours. It was so much work for Mother to take care of her in addition to her other children. Mother was afraid of having other retarded children, and when she became pregnant twice again, she made herself have two miscarriages. For all these years, she had carried the guilt of those horrible acts. This led to nervous problems and several nervous breakdowns, including a stay in the mental hospital. She was under a doctor's care for years. How Satan tormented her and made her think that God would not forgive her for what she had done. What a burden she carried all those years!

During the time of caring for my mother, I reached my greatest point of despair and fatigue, even wishing to die. Even people in the Bible, on occasions, wished to die. Remember Jonah saying, "And it came to pass, when the sun did arise, that God prepared a vehement east wind; and the sun beat upon the head of Jonah, that he fainted, and wished in himself to die, and said, 'It is better for me to die than to live'" (Jonah 4:8).

During these years of hell, Mother always wanted to be right under my feet. Even while she was in the hospital, I had to stay with her. She tried to dominate my life and the lives of Elias and Ricky.

One cold day in January my mother had been acting nervously, walking the floor and becoming mentally unstable. She came to my bedroom at eight in the morning. The woman who had helped us with Mother for five years arrived at our home at 8:15 A.M. Between 8:00 A.M. and 8:15

A.M., my mother left the house, entered the back-yard, walked to the creek, jumped in, came back to the house and was at our door waiting for this woman to come. When the aide came in, my wet and muddy mother walked behind her. My mother admitted that she had tried to commit suicide by jumping into the creek behind our house. She said that every time she would put her head under the water, an angel of God would physically jerk her head back up. She tried to kill herself several times and every time the angel of God would prevent it. My mother was quite old and unable to climb up and over the bulkhead that was placed between the creek and our back-yard. Doing that would have been impossible for her apart from divine assistance.

What could I do? I put her into the bathtub with warm water and washed her. Then, I walked down behind the house to look. I saw where she had come out. I saw that the rocks and the cement of the bulkhead were still wet and muddy. How could I have ever gotten over her drowning? How messed up and sickly she had to be to do this to herself! I called the doctor and took her to the hospital. The doctor discovered that medication had caused her to become very unstable mentally.

In those years my mother frequently would be rushed to the hospital, especially for heart fail-ure. She had been at death's door more times than can be counted. Doctors repeatedly thought that she would not make it out of the hospital.

Yet, she always did.

One time when she became very sick, we brought her to the hospital and for three days I took care of her every minute. I did this so much that I did not have time for coffee or sleep. During these three days, she continued to cough and have diarrhea. My mother became so sick that I was forced to hold her on the bed and keep the IV in her arm.

At the end of the third day, the doctor came into my mother's room and told me that he could not find out what was wrong with her. He could not help her. Whatever was wrong or whatever type of sickness she had seemed to be killing her. Again I cried out to God. The Lord told me that it was a bird fever and gave me the name for it. I told the doctor what God had said. The doctor looked at me very strangely, turned around and hurried out. About one hour later he came back into the room and said that he did not have time to check out that she had bird fever, but that she had all the symptoms. Because she was dying, he had no time to run the necessary tests. I said, "Go ahead and treat her for that and I will take the responsibility!" He had to quarantine us. The Lord finally delivered my mother from the bird fever a few days later. I was exhausted after this stage of the battle, but the fight for my mother was still not over.

Satan, knowing that I could go no further, prompted my sister Sue to call the hospital and curse me for everything in the book. Finally, I

knew that I could go no further. So again I began
to cry out to God, "What is wrong that I have to go
through this by myself? Lord, I can't go another
night without sleep!" The Lord spoke and said,
"You have not because you ask not!" It did not
take me long to ask Him for help. In about ten
minutes, the telephone rang with a friend calling
to see if I needed help.

Mother got to where she would suffer insomnia until about five o'clock in the morning.
During this time, she would call out all night
long. Elias and I began to pray about that. We
would go into her room and cry out to God for
her night after night. Nevertheless, it seemed
that we would get through one thing only to be
faced by another.

All of this was going on while Elias and I cried
out to God for our son's healing as well. We also
went anywhere that a revival was taking place so
that godly men or women who had the gifts of the
Holy Spirit working through them could pray for
Ricky. I wanted someone to touch God for our
son. Money and denominations don't matter
when you need something from God badly
enough.

The barrage of problems that Satan instigated
within both our families became so horrible that
they literally began to destroy all hope for our
son to be healed. Satan's purpose was to tie Elias
and me down, weaken us so that our attention
was turned away from the miracle that awaited
our son. These storms were causing so much

the church to see if any older people were standing around, intending to give my seat to them, but something stronger than myself kept me in my seat. When the minister came to the platform, he said, "I said I was going to preach on the battle of Armageddon if the Lord let me! Yet, God changed my text when I came into this church! It is for this young lady sitting right here! I am going to teach you how to pray tonight! God has called you to be an intercessor! He called you to pray for other people! He loves someone else besides you and your bunch! He wants you to put your family on the altar and leave them there!"

God had done what I had asked Him to do. He had confirmed what He wanted me to do. Have you ever laid someone on the altar when Satan was trying to kill him or her? Have you ever had to sit back and watch God work instead of getting involved? I did not quite understand what the Lord meant at first about laying them on the altar and leaving them there. I remember many days and nights when I would have to hang up the telephone. I did not know what to do and neither did I know what was happening. There had been one thing after another in our lives for so long. So much horror had taken place that when the telephone rang, I began to tremble. I would then hang the telephone up, go back, lie on the bed and weep violently. I finally understood that by placing my family upon the altar, I was surrendering them into God's hands and turning my attention firmly toward praying for my son first and then others.

These were just some of the storms we had to endure. Always one problem would begin before another problem ended. There was never a time that could be considered a time of peace. At these times I would pray and be led into fasts from three to twenty-one days in order to break through the barriers of the demonic. Praying and fasting helped! Apart from both praying and fasting, we might not have survived to tell the history of our lives and relate what God has done.

Chapter Four

RECEIVING A MIRACLE

In 1975 I experienced something beyond expectation that was humbling and yet almost indescribable. I was praying on my knees in our extra room, which had become our prayer room. Nothing was out of the ordinary until I felt the Spirit of God rush into the room and overshadow me. Then, I was given a vision. I saw one of the same wheels that Ezekiel described in the first and tenth chapters of Ezekiel. This wheel-angel came rolling into my room early in the morning. The wheel was actually a type of angel, sent by God to deliver a message of hope and promise. This angel broke through the demonic layers that bound and imprisoned us.

The angel appeared as a wheel within a wheel. He had the appearance of an inner and outer wheel attached by a joint to make one individual wheel. There were four sides and the angel could go in any direction he chose without turning. His color was that of amber. The rings of the wheel were full of eyes. The angel had the ability to speak, and his voice was as the voice of many waters all sounding in sequence. The glory of God that surrounded him lit up the room. While I had envisioned angels before this event, I had never seen any like this. I have never forgotten it. The entire miracle of my son's healing is founded upon this vision. It became our lifeline because all that God gave to us afterward was used to confirm this vision.

In the midst of this, I saw a sickle in a large wheat field cutting down wheat even though no one was operating it. There were large storehouses that were being filled to the brim. The angel spoke to me and said, "The wheat field is the world of sinners; the sickle going about cutting down the wheat is the End-Time harvest. The storehouses are the churches who are alive, giving the Holy Spirit a place in their services. These storehouses will be filled to the brim." I felt that the Lord, through His angel, promised another Great Awakening in the End Times, which would take place before the Rapture of the church.

Since I was not a biblical scholar, I did not understand the "wheel" when I saw it. I did not know that it was a very powerful angel, or that Ezekiel had seen four of these wheels himself more than 2,500 years ago. I was truly upset, not knowing whether I was crazy or moving into the realm of fanaticism. The church that I attended, though believing in the gifts of the Holy Spirit, visions, dreams and other manifestations, had not been taken as deeply as I was going.

I prayed for help and God led me to call my sister-in-law, Evelyn Roberts Cox. She was, and still is, a Church of God minister. When I told her what had happened, she informed me that what I had seen was found in the Bible. I had unknowingly explained the wheel exactly as Ezekiel had seen it. I was confused and asked her why the angel had also shown me a man and said, "This is for you," when I already had a husband. She told me that this was not what the wheel angel meant. She said, "Hold on to the Lord, let nothing divert you from the goal set before you by God. Whatever was going on was truly of God so that you would hang on." She also said to wait and allow God to unravel the mystery about the man. I waited and within three weeks what the angel had spoken about a man did come to pass.

On Sunday, at the last point of this three-week period, I could hardly contain myself. I could not be still! It felt as if I had fire in my bones. Did not Jeremiah say, "His Word was in mine heart as a burning fire shut up in my bones, and I was weary with forbearing, and I could not stay" (Jeremiah 20:9)?

I tried to read a Christian book, and the more I read, the more I would burn, and then the more nervous I would be. It was so bad that Elias told me to go to the hospital to find out what was going on. None of the doctors or the nurses could find anything wrong with me and sent me home. As I drove home, I turned on the radio and heard an advertisement about a tent revival taking place nearby that night. As I was listening to the radio, I felt the Lord's call to go.

When I got there, standing on the platform was the man I had seen in the vision three weeks earlier. Then he took the microphone and said, "My meeting here in Jacksonville is over." I thought to myself that I had just gotten there. Then, the evangelist said, "A prophet is coming into Jacksonville and will use my tent to hold a revival. If this man tells you that you are going to die, you better make your funeral arrangements!" The prophet was Billy Jo Fain, a former bank robber who had been on the FBI's ten most wanted list. The evangelist continued by saying that this man had been tried and sentenced to a ninety-nine year prison sentence. Yet his praying mother cried out to God, reminding Him that even before his birth her son had been called to be a prophet. She cried out to God that the life he was living was not what was promised. Miraculously, God set this man free from his term and he became a minister for God.

When it was time for the evangelist to pray for people, he called me up out of the audience and told me to lay hands upon others. Later, he told me that he saw from the pulpit that I was engulfed in a flame of fire and needed to pray for the people there who were in need. I found out that praying for people was the only way the anointing of God could be released within me and its power diminished within my bones. The fire that I was feeling was God's anointing that needed an outlet. I had never been taught that the anointing needs a channel for release. This release comes only by praying for others, especially with the laying on of hands. When I prayed for others, the burning lessened and would stop temporarily. It would then come back as God directed me to pray for more people.

I came home and told Elias and Ricky what had happened. Elias immediately said, "There will be false prophets before the End Time deceiving many! We must guard ourselves against all deception! We will not go!" I spoke to him very calmly and said, "You may not go, but the Lord is dealing with me. I am going!" When it comes right down to it, we must obey God rather than men. Peter and the other apostles had to make that same choice. Acts 5:29 says, "We ought to obey God rather than men." Elias had not seen the vision and did not have the conviction of the Holy Spirit to go to the tent revival. He was worried about me going off the deep end, following false prophets and false teachers. We finally agreed to "lay out a fleece" before God as the saints in the Old Testament had done when they did not know the exact will of God for themselves or their nation. (See Deuteronomy 18:4; Judges 6:37–40; Job 31:20.) We prayed that if this prophet was from God, he would call all three of us out at once and pray for us. Since I had never seen that happen before, it seemed like a good test to determine whether he was of God or not.

On a Wednesday morning, Billy Jo Fain had

his first service in that old tent. I drove there in a separate car from Elias and Ricky. All three of us sat in different locations inside. We were "trying the spirits," just as John had warned all saints to do. (See 1 John 4:1–3.)

When this prophet came up on the platform to preach, he looked at my son and said, "Young man, you have a learning disability. Can I pray for you?" He then pointed to Elias and said, "This is your son! Come up here!" Next, he turned to his left and pointed to me saying, "Come up here! All three of you are a family!" He told us to join hands. Then he told us about our life and how Satan had conspired against our home from the moment Ricky was conceived. He described all that had been happening to us, repeated that we had been in eight wrecks and even described the alarm clock going off every thirty minutes for the first six years of Ricky's life.

He continued to exhort us with several other words from the Lord for all of us. There were eleven points in all: 1) Ricky is ordained of God; 2) he is consecrated and dedicated unto God; 3) he is terribly retarded with no hope, except from the Lord; 4) he will be in the world but not of it; 5) the Lord will heal him very shortly so that He can use him for an End-Time harvest; 6) God Himself will educate Ricky; 7) God had brought us out of our church because He did not want Ricky to be contaminated by tradition; 8) God would not allow Ricky to be taught by traditional methods and strategies; 9) God would allow

Ricky to go to college, but Ricky would end up teaching there; 10) Ricky would learn the Bible from the ancient languages and from the history of the ancient church; 11) Ricky would turn the church world upside down.

I am so glad that I didn't have to unlearn erroneous doctrine about the prophetic word. Many believe that prophecy is universal and is only given to a whole nation or a whole congregation rather than to an individual. What good is the prophetic word for edification if it is only universal? What does the saint do when he is crying out for God to give him some direction and the church says there is no specific word for him? There are many instances in the Bible where prophetic words were not given to a nation, but to an individual person. Ahab, David and Paul are just a few examples among many others. (See 1 Kings 21:11–22:53; Jeremiah 11:21; 14:14; Ezekiel 29:2; 37:2; 38:2; 1 Samuel 9:1–27; 2 Chronicles 15:3; Nehemiah 6:12; Proverbs 30:1; 31:1; 2 Chronicles 18:7; 20:37; John 11:51; Isaiah 7:14; Jude 14; 1 Kings 1; 11:29–43; 13:18–20; 14:2; 16:7; Acts 21:1–13; 2 Samuel 7:8–17; 12:1–8.)

It was Billy Joe Fain who gave prophetic words that were directed to this family. He spoke mighty words about our family's part in the End-Time harvest and about our ministry being based in Jacksonville. After receiving several prophetic words that morning, my husband cried out to God and asked, "Why? Why? Why? Why were we chosen to receive the promise and the blessings?"

At the revival the next morning, the prophet called him out and answered his question. "It is not you. It is God's sovereignty and especially His grace!"

I had the vision of the wheel angel a little more than three weeks before this experience. This man was the first prophet that I had seen and his prophetic word was the first that I had ever heard. Since prophecy was new to me, I could do nothing but believe. I had nothing else to hold on to except the prophecy and the vision that God had given. This prophecy confirmed that vision. Both of these were like an immovable log in the midst of a mighty river that provided a secure place for a drowning victim to hold. That's just what I did. I held on tightly to the vision and the prophecy. It saved me from drowning in a river of hopelessness. I am very glad that Billy Jo Fain lived long enough to see God heal and educate Ricky.

During this same time, the tent revival gave birth to other revivals in Jacksonville and Fernandina, which are still in effect. This great tent revival is where Ricky experienced the baptism of the Holy Spirit and heard the voice of God speak to him audibly. Billy Joe Fain told Ricky that God wanted to speak to him as a friend talks to another friend, face-to-face. After hearing this, Ricky went home, went to bed and waited. Finally God was able to break through the demonic barrier that had tried to prevent Ricky from hearing God. For that next twenty-four hour period, Ricky heard the audible voice of God. His room was so filled with God's glory, that smoke visibly filled the room. God spoke many things to him that night. This was not the last time that Ricky was granted the privilege of hearing the audible voice of God for twenty-four hours.

After this, Ricky was given his first vision. He saw heaven open and the hands of God coming down and breaking through the dark clouds. Underneath the hands the words were written, "For I shall bring forth truth out of darkness for the sake of my people." The Lord told him that this would be the logo for his ministry.

Several other manifestations of the Lord happened to others during this time. The first manifestation was a blue mist. It covered the tent visibly, flowing around and touching my sister Sue three separate times. As the mist passed over the heads of the people, many fell out as if they were dead.

The second manifestation happened to a coworker of mine when she attended the revival. Though she had never gone to a Pentecostal revival, she would never forget this one. She accepted the Lord as her Savior and experienced one of the most severe cases of being "drunk in the Spirit" that I have ever seen in my life. She stayed this way for five straight days. At work I saw her stagger from one side of the hall to the other saying, "Be not drunk with wine but with the Spirit saith the Lord!" Needless to say, I was begging God to lift the Spirit from her. So many people from all over the mill were coming to see what was going on that my boss asked me to lift whatever was on her. I replied that if this was of God, everything would work out and no one would be harmed. Her testimony resulted in much repentance and deliverance at work.

The third manifestation was the visible sighting of an angel. One night a man appeared in front of the tent. He spoke with such wisdom and had such a holy appearance that there was no question that he was an angel. His appearance was absolutely beautiful. Why did he come? I had been studying the demonic even though I was not yet mature enough to handle the topic of demons. When a saint studies demons, evil spirits will congregate around. Therefore, the saint had better know how to fight them. The first thing that I told the angel was that I was studying demons. He replied, "Why study demons? Study angels! They help the saints." I was dumbfounded. I had thought that studying demons was a mark of maturity. I learned so much from our conversation. The last thing I asked was, "Can we pray for you?" He humbly bowed his head and accepted our prayer. Since then, this same man has appeared in two visions, proclaiming himself as an angel of the Lord and coming in the name of the Lord. From our conversation, I found out that he believed that Jesus Christ was born from a virgin, was crucified and arose from the grave. He also proclaimed that Jesus Christ is God, and he accepted all the fundamental doctrines of Christianity. Remember Hebrews 13:2.

Elias also had two notable experiences with

the Lord. The first can only be described as amazing. It was not a vision or a dream, but what can only be called a "translation" or "a rapture." In this, a person is either caught up bodily as were Enoch, Elijah and Philip or his soul is caught up without the body. (See Genesis 5:24; 2 Kings 2:9–12; Acts 8:39.)

Elias' soul was not caught up to heaven, but to the valley near the mountain where the body of Moses was buried. As he turned and looked, numerous people were sitting down in countless ranks doing nothing at all. He saw only a few workers running up the mountain and back down to the valley, gathering the gifts and the blessings that God has for all saints. A mighty angel appeared at the top of the mountain. When the feet of this angel landed upon the mountain, blue sparks went everywhere and illuminated the land and the sky. His appearance was so bright with light and glory that nothing on this earth can describe it. This brightness spread forth from the mountain down to the valley. Elias had never seen such a beautiful creature. Words cannot truly describe angels.

Though Elias was far away, the angel said to him audibly, "Come!" Elias got up from where he was sitting and began to walk toward the angel. The angel said, "No," and pointed his finger while Elias continued to float toward him. Finally, Elias reached the angel who, by his power, set him down. At that point the angel said, "All those people who were shown to be doing nothing for the sake of Christ have been sitting right in the place where they were saved. They have not moved an inch. If these people are not extremely careful, they will be sitting right there when Jesus comes! All the gifts and blessings for my people are found up here upon this mountain if they will come!" This profound statement still echoes in our minds as Elias shares this experience from the Lord. We have never forgotten these words. It has motivated us to continually strive to answer His call.

Before this translation ended, the angel showed Elias that Ricky was upon the mountain where the gifts and blessings were, receiving a hedge of protection around him. All of us had prayed all week before this experience that God would do just that.

Symbolically, the mountain is heaven and the valley is the earth. The few coming up and down are those who, through prayers and beseeching God, have entered heaven and received the gifts and blessings of the Lord.

The second and last experience during this time happened when Elias was coming home from shopping. He drove down Broward Road as he often did with nothing appearing out of the ordinary. As he approached our home, he stopped behind a car. Instead of going around it, he sat waiting. The Lord spoke audibly and suddenly, "Look up!" He looked up and saw a speeding car traveling at sixty-five miles per hour behind him. He had only enough time to say, "Jesus help me!" before his car was hit. As he said those words, a blue mist entered his car and surrounded him. The mist was visible and tangible. Elias got out of the vehicle and said, "Well, Lord, it is yours if you want Satan to tear it up!" A police officer heard what he said and thought he was in shock. A friend, who happened to be present, said to the police officer, "He's all right. He is a praying man and believes that the Lord has preserved him through this." That's exactly what God did! The car was totaled, but Elias was fine.

Ricky was fourteen years old when this prophecy was given. Having received this assurance, I became bold in the Lord. I went everywhere telling everyone that God was going to heal my son. People looked at me strangely. They thought that I was crazy and pitied me. Many laughed at me during the two-year time period before Ricky's miracle. Even my family did not understand what was going on. One of my sisters called after Ricky had graduated from college, crying and asking forgiveness. She could not understand with her finite mind what a marvelous and mighty miracle God had wrought within our family.

Too often we seek and beg God for miracles and then, when they come to our families, we reject them or deny that they ever came at all. Only by the grace of God does He still perform miracles, even in the midst of our denial and rejections. Thank God for His grace!

Chapter Five

AFTERMATH OF A MIRACLE

Between 1975 and December of 1977, Elias and I continued to have Ricky tutored every Saturday, even during the summer. Even though we had received God's promise, we did not stand idly by doing nothing. We kept holding on to that promise! It was all that we had. There were very few signs that God was working to fulfill His words to us about Ricky. Yet, He was working behind the scenes, placing pieces of the puzzle together. He showed His true mastery and handiwork, demonstrating that He is truly the Great Architect.

In December of 1977, the life of Ricky was instantaneously and totally changed. The three of us went to a Full Gospel revival at another church. The preacher, Al Edenfield, sang and sang. As he was singing, he went back to where Ricky was sitting and said, "Young man, you have a learning disability! Can I pray for you?" Ricky replied yes.

The preacher put his hand on the head of Ricky then snatched it back saying, "The Lord has heard your cries as you lay awake at night saying, 'Why can't I learn like other children?' If your mother will stand on faith and put you in the tenth grade, God will fill in the foundation!" These words so struck me that I became paralyzed all over. I could not think or realize what God had just done. Words cannot describe the state in which I found myself. However, thank God, the preacher knew that I did not understand or fully realize what had happened to my son that very night and instant! As I was going out the door he said, "Little sister, you did not understand what happened to your son! The Lord said that He has healed your son! In three days, University Christian School will call you to take him out of that school. The teachers cannot help him and are using him as a babysitter in his class." I knew that this was true because a teacher had told me this. I did not become excited over what the preacher had said because I was in shock.

I continued to feel as if I was in a fog until the school called me three days later. The elementary principal, Mrs. Sanders, was on the phone. She said that I screamed out to her, "Mrs. Sanders, the Lord has healed my boy! Put him in the tenth grade! I will be over there in a few minutes!" Although the school was thirty minutes away, I flew there, breaking the speed limit. I ran into the school yelling out loudly, "God has healed my son!" Can you imagine what Mrs. Sanders was thinking? She thought that I had lost it and was having a nervous breakdown over my son. She sent me to the head principal of the school who was her husband. I told him the same thing that I had said to her. Of course, at first he did not believe that God had healed my son. He said, "Mrs. Roberts, you are going to destroy your son! Jumping seven grades is impossible for anyone! This school has done all that it can do!" Then I noticed a Bible verse on the wall. It read, "But Jesus beheld them, and said unto them, With men this is impossible; but with God all things are possible (Matthew 19:26)." I told him very kindly, but with holy boldness, "Mr. Sanders, if you don't believe that my son fits in that verse, take it down because you are a hypocrite!" Mr. Sanders wanted me to send Ricky to a psychologist named Dr. Smith to have him analyzed. I said, "There is no problem with this. I have had Ricky analyzed by so many psychologists and psychiatrists that another doesn't bother me." When I told him to call his doctor, he then made an appointment.

When I saw Dr. Smith, the very first thing I told him was that God had healed Ricky. Dr. Smith said to me, "I do not believe in that junk!" The doctor had already been informed about Ricky and his learning disability. I said to him, "I am a believer and God's work can be tested! I want you to test God's work, whatever the cost!"

A few days later, Mrs. Dugger and I went for a

consultation on the test results. Dr. Smith said, "I don't know what to tell you people! Put this boy in the tenth grade by all means! He was doing algebra, trigonometry and all other tenth grade work that he had never had!"

The Sanders did not want to place Ricky in the tenth grade unless it was agreed that he would remain on trial there for the rest of the school year until it could be verified that he could really do the work. They knew that on or before December of 1977, Ricky had only been working at a third-grade level. Between Christmas vacation and the beginning of the next semester, Ricky prepared himself to enter the tenth grade. His special education class remained his homeroom. It was a life or death matter for Ricky. His whole future hung in the balance. It was time for God's work to be truly tested!

Although God had miraculously worked in Ricky, the teachers did not want a retarded student in their classes, even on trial. They could not comprehend that God had healed my son and still labeled Ricky retarded. This was a terrible problem for Ricky, but it was no problem for God. Several months before God healed Ricky, a teacher named Mr. Hazlett moved from Pennsylvania to be a history teacher. He agreed to have a retarded child in his class since he himself was the father of a child with a handicap. Elias and I saw God's hand in working out these details. Each special education teacher also had a part in this miracle and played valuable roles in God's workings.

After nine weeks on trial, Mr. Hazlett called me to talk. He said, "The first Monday morning after the Christmas vacation Ricky came into my classroom. The other students, knowing that he was retarded, began to laugh at him. His face and eyes were downcast and he began to tremble. I put him in the front of the classroom where he took out his notebook and began to write down everything that I wrote on the blackboard. I went very slowly in explaining the lesson. That first week there was a test on the subject material and Ricky scored one hundred. In six weeks he was tutoring many of the other students who had made fun of him."

During this probationary period, other teachers also decided to allow Ricky in their classrooms after Mr. Hazlett's experience. They all had to hand in regular reports, in addition to his report card, on his progress. At the end of the first nine weeks, Mrs. Sanders called me crying and said, "I think you need to read the reports of the teachers!" As I drove up to the school, Mrs. Sanders met me with a smile on her face. She gave me a teacher's report that read, "Mrs. Sanders, this report concerns Ricky Roberts who has a ninety-six average in my class. He is a well-behaved young man. Do you have any more special education students like Ricky? Please send them to my class!" In that half of the year, Ricky not only learned how to diagram sentences, but made the honor roll as well.

I will never forget another day that Mrs.

Sanders called me excited about Ricky. All the time that he was in the special education class she had never heard him laugh. That day she had heard him laugh out loud for the first time. She said that she felt like Ricky had discovered a long lost continent.

It is impossible to explain the joy Elias and I felt when we came home from work and found Ricky doing his homework. He was never as happy as when he turned sixteen, knowing that Jesus healed him.

When the school year ended, I went to Mrs. Sanders and asked for their best English teacher to tutor Ricky over the summer. She said that she would trust Ricky with only one teacher, Mrs. Glidden. She had taught college and also worked for a book company as their main editor. I knew that she was the person that we needed to work with him. That summer she tutored Ricky five times. During four of these times she taught four different levels of English to him: elementary, junior high school, high school, and two years of college. The fifth time she spent two hours testing him to see whether he had learned it. She came through the living room with her hands in the air praising Jesus about what He had done for Ricky.

Ricky entered the tenth grade for credit in the 1978–1979 school year. The teachers were strictly grading him, making sure that they all had the same high standards for him. They wanted to make sure that he was truly earning his grades.

The very first day Ricky was called into the

principal's office and told that he would have to take U.S. history for tenth-grade credit. Miss Cover, who taught this subject, was extremely hard. No one had ever made a grade higher than a C in her class. She planned on going to graduate school to be a lawyer. Ricky told the principal, "God has not healed me to run from anyone! Give her to me!"

I overheard Ricky on the phone one day talking to Miss Cover about his report card. He said, "Miss Cover, I have averaged my grade and I have a B! My report card said that I had a C." Miss Cover acknowledged her mistake and changed his grade the next day. Ricky kept on working until he made two A's in her class.

Finding Ricky on his knees early in the morning was still very common. He often prayed himself to sleep. Sometimes his legs would be asleep, and we would have to help him into bed. While God gave Ricky the ability to learn, He also demanded that he study. Ricky applied himself to his academic subjects relentlessly. It was as if he had an unquenchable thirst for knowledge that continues to this day.

That year, he was nominated for membership in the National Honor Society. He passed the entire year with four A's and four B's. Elias and I received that report card with an unspeakable joy. For so many years, Satan had worked to prevent Ricky from learning, but God made it possible. I thank God we believed Him and not Satan!

In the summer Ricky began to teach himself about computers. This was a skill he would need very badly later on as God walked our family through what He wanted for our lives.

In the eleventh grade, Ricky was initiated into the National Honor Society with a beautiful candlelight service. Mrs. Bishop, the sponsor, said that night, "Lord, I am thankful for my son, but no one could be as thankful as the parents of Ricky are!"

For the first time in his life, Ricky could hold his head up high with joy on his face. Satan had lied to Ricky for all those years, but God continued to speak the truth. In the eleventh grade Ricky averaged seven A's and one B.

In the twelfth grade, he took business law as a subject. The teacher, Mrs. Richardson, had been a substitute teacher in his special education class a few years before God had healed Ricky. She couldn't remember if she had ever taught him before at University Christian School. Ricky reminded her of the class he had been in. As she recalled this she was dumbfounded. Her only memory of Ricky in that class was his struggle to pronounce the word *and*. Now, he was taking business law, pronouncing twelfth-grade words and defining them.

As a senior, he also studied "Old English" as part of a literature class. I could not understand why God would want Ricky to take this. I now know what God's sovereign purpose was in having him do this. Most of the books that we have bought are written in an ancient English style that only Ricky can understand!

In 1981, Ricky received the International Youth in Achievement of the World award. Only ten thousand teenagers are inducted annually. Again in 1982, during his first year of college, he received the same award.

The night Ricky graduated from high school he received every award but two. When he went up to receive his first award, the principal told Ricky, "Just stay up here, you will walk yourself to death!" He earned the highest grade average ever achieved in business law, was Class Honor Student and Best Student in Religion. Elias and I had prayed that Jesus would receive glory and honor. That night Ricky also received the Outstanding Award. The principal asked, "Why is Ricky receiving the Outstanding Award? I don't think that he will mind if I tell you that when he came to this school he was mentally retarded and in our special education class for about five years. Ricky told me that as his faith in the Lord Jesus Christ grew, his learning disability was healed! It does appear that this is true since he jumped seven grades, an impossibility without God stepping into the situation!" After the graduation ceremony people gathered around Ricky wanting to know what had happened. The Lord received the entire honor and glory that night because of His grace in Ricky's life.

After the graduation ceremony, the Lord spoke to Ricky saying, "I have taken you from the tail and made you the head. Now, Ricky, I want you to go on a fast!" This was a difficult time to go without food because we had a garden and were harvesting our fresh vegetables. At first, Elias and I did not know how long the fast would be. After twenty-one days had passed, we became upset. We began to cry and pray that God would help Ricky. Elias would push his plate of food away and cry out to God to allow him to do the fasting for Ricky. Ricky fasted for forty days without anything to eat, drinking only water. What was so amazing about this fast was that one day before the end of this fast, God told Ricky that since he was obedient, he could eat anything immediately after the fast was over and it would not hurt him in the least. Ricky told his father and me what God had said. Ricky wanted to eat a steak, French fries, salad, and bread and drink tea. Elias and I knew that eating so much was not recommended after a long fast, but we obeyed the voice of God and cooked Ricky all that he had asked. When the fast was over, Ricky sat down and ate all that we had prepared for him, suffering no harm. Obedience is truly better than sacrifice.

When Ricky began to go to college, he attended a junior college here in Jacksonville. I told the counselor about what God had done in the healing of my son. She said meanly, "He will earn his grades here!" I responded, "He had better earn it! At that high school, I paid for his education and it was not given to him in the least!" When he was tested, he placed in the second year of college. He went there until the middle of his second year.

Before he finished, the Lord spoke to him and said, "Come out of that college because you have learned all that I want you to know there. Your mother is not going to like this, but I want you to study the Bible and the books that I tell you to buy." What God wanted was truly a shock! I thought that Ricky would get a degree in computer science, but the Father had other plans for him. I was not going to get between God and my son. That would have been dangerous. I told him to go and buy the books that God led him to buy. In about an hour, he came out with a list of books. I turned off dinner, and we went to a Baptist bookstore. The manager had never heard of these books.

Again, we found ourselves praying and crying to God. I asked God if we were descending into fanaticism. We went to other bookstores where the managers also had never heard of these books. All the way to work I could do nothing but cry and pray to God again. The next day the Lord led me to call a church in Oklahoma. At first, I found no help, but God said to me, "Try again!" This time I got through and told the woman on the telephone the story about God healing my son. She gave me the name of a man whose professional name was "the Book Finder." I called him and he not only knew about the books, but also agreed to help Ricky find them. God helped us find all the books, and we then bought them. Later God opened other doors and means by which Ricky could find other books. Right before my eyes the prophecy given when Ricky was fourteen years old was being fulfilled.

During this time, I would come home from work and find Ricky reading with twenty or twenty-five books on the living room floor around him. He could summarize each page and remember what subject had been discussed on a certain page. It was common for Ricky to come into our bedroom at about three or four in the morning to wake us up and tell us what he had found out from his studies.

The Lord did not always make it easy on us to find the book that he would tell Ricky to buy. Once the Lord told him to buy a book, and we tried everywhere but could not find it. Ricky began to cry and pray to God. He told the Lord, "My father and mother will buy the book if we can find it. Help us." The Lord said, "Ricky, tell your mother to quit fretting! Call the Library of Congress and have them reprint it!" The Library of Congress made a loose-leaf copy for us, which we had permanently bound.

One night after about five years of studying the books that God told him to buy, Ricky was praying around midnight. He cried out to the Lord because he felt led to get a doctorate but knew that no college would accept his unorthodox education. The Lord responded to him by saying, "Render therefore unto Caesar things which are Caesar's, and unto God the things that are God's." Ricky said, "Father, are You telling me that I can go to college?" The Lord said yes to his desire and not long afterward showed him a college in North Carolina that would take him.

When Ricky started Christian Bible College, the president gave him a year of college free if he would do research for them. Ricky agreed. The officers of that college said that they did not teach Ricky; he taught the college. Remember the prophecy!

Ricky spent nine years there and received doctorates in theology, Greek, Hebrew, Aramaic and Latin, and a Ph.D. in Old Testament and New Testament studies. He graduated summa cum laude and was the first student to graduate from Christian Bible College with a 4.00 GPA. Between 1982 and 2003, Ricky received numerous other awards, such as Community Leaders of America (1983), Young Personalities of the South (1983), Young Personalities of America (1983), Biographical Roll of Honor (1984), International Book of Honor (1985), Who's Who in America (1998), 1,000 Great Americans (2002) and Who's Who in the World (2000–2003).

I have been asked so many times what I would have done with my son if God had not healed him. That is a place I do not want to go. I see nothing but grace in the miracle wrought for my son. That grace can come upon anyone if he or she will meet God halfway. That is all that God ever requires. When I do ponder that question, there is absolutely no regret over his life. His father and I treasured him and were proud of him even before God healed him. We believe that God gives only the best gifts to His children. Satan is the one who damages and destroys, tempting us into the consequences of rebellion.

When asked to describe this miracle of God healing his mind, Ricky replies, "It is like living in a very dark tunnel for years. Then, suddenly, a match is lit. The small light from this match becomes brighter and brighter until finally the light engulfs the whole tunnel." In his life, all of this was done in an instant, through the power of God working internally upon his brain. Not until Dr. Smith tested Ricky did we have any proof that God had done anything. Still, Elias, Ricky, and I held on!

Time and again, Ricky has flashbacks about his sixteen years of retardation. A certain smell, image, taste, touch or sound can bring all of those memories back in a flood. God desires that Ricky will never forget his state of retardation. For years Ricky has suffered from a recurring nightmare. He finds himself sitting in a high school classroom, unable to read a word, failing an important test and not graduating. Only when Ricky wakes up, does he realize that it was only a dream. In the last three years this nightmare finally disappeared when Ricky took authority over it. Satan used this dream to torment my son. Thank God the saints have the victory and power over Satan through the blood of Christ in every realm.

Even before Ricky's healing and nine years of higher education, he was enrolled in the school of the Spirit, learning from the Holy Spirit about the spiritual gifts and how they must be used. From this age to the present, Ricky has been used greatly in the prophetic ministry, giving words of edification and comfort to the brokenhearted. God works gifts of healing and miracles through him as well. Ricky, in his state of retardation, could not reach up to God, but God could reach down to him, using the gifts of the Holy Spirit through him.

Between 1975 and 2003, the Lord granted Ricky many supernatural experiences. Besides hearing the audible voice of God two notable times, Ricky has visibly seen the wings of angels flying across his room. He has seen the glory of God in such intensity that it lit up his whole room and almost blinded him for a time. He has heard heavenly sounds that cannot be described or uttered by a human voice. He has smelled the sweet odors of heaven enter his room and the hellish odors of demons as well. He has had countless visions that include the Lord, angels and demons, among other things. In visions, my son has seen heaven and hell, and even the very throne room of God.

Ricky and I will chronicle these visions and other experiences in a later book. The most vivid time we'll recount is during a twenty-two day fast when the very presence of hell entered his room for eight of those days. I will never forget it!

Chapter Six

TESTIMONIES AND PROOFS OF A MIRACLE

A Statement From a Thankful Mother
By Dorothy Roberts

I am just a country mother who loved her family and had only a simple and uneducated faith. I knew only enough to believe what I read in the Bible. No preacher, teacher, theologian or any other scholar could take the words of life from my hands and from my life when it came down to my son.

I can say that all that I knew about prayer was to end it in the name of Jesus. What I learned about intercession came from none but the Holy Spirit. It was He who led me all the way and upon whom I rested my faith and my case.

The parts of this book written by me contain my thoughts in my own style. The style is like me, simple and straightforward. By staying true to myself, I pray that this style will touch the heart of those in a state of hopelessness.

I encourage all seekers of truth and all who feel hopeless to reach out to God for the answer, to step out into the deep waters of our faith, to lay down tradition and listen to God rather than man. What God did for my family, He is well able to do for all!

A Statement From a Pastor by Jeana Tomlinson, Co-Pastor, New Covenant Ministries of Jacksonville, Florida

When I first met Dot Roberts, she did not know who I was. She was testifying to my son about the good things that God had done for her own son, Ricky. Tears streamed down her face as she recalled all the years that she had interceded for a miracle of God for her boy. I was so captivated by her sincerity that I listened intently for the duration of her testimony. I stood spellbound by her account of the three years of desperate weeping, which preceded one of the greatest miracles I have ever heard. Then, I assured her that I indeed felt that God had brought us together. She spoke as a modern-day Hannah, weeping centuries ago for a son that she could give back to God. In her desperation, God came through and granted her the desire of her heart.

My desire is that you will be as blessed as I am by the mighty deeds done in the mind and heart of Dr. Ricky. You will be particularly impressed at the significant role his mother, Dot, has played in the final orchestration of one of the most spectacular signs and wonders of our day.

Does God still heal? Yes!

Will He do it for you? Absolutely!

Read and study this account and permit the God of the miraculous to move in your life. Learn from Dot's walk through tears how to summon the Sovereign. *Jesus Christ the same yesterday, and today, and forever* (Hebrews 13:8).

MEMORIES OF A TEACHER
BY SALLY YOUNG

I first met Ricky at University Christian School in Jacksonville, Florida, in 1973. I was the Special Education teacher there and taught both the mentally handicapped as well as those who were significantly behind in their academics. At the time, Ricky was coming to our school from a regular sixth grade class in the public schools. I tested him, and he was only reading on a primer level, which is well below first grade.

Ricky was very sweet natured, wanted to learn and had a desire to serve God. He loved the Lord. I remember one time I asked the students to give sacrificially to some missionaries, and we had a little box to put their offerings in. Everyone gave a little, but I remember Ricky gave all that he had. He was always that way. He was always loving, giving and caring. You could tell how much God was already working in his heart even at that young age.

I had Ricky in my class that year and the next. We labored every day on reading, language and math skills. I knew I could help him, but I did not think he would ever catch up to his grade level. His mother would even bring him over to my house to be privately tutored in reading because she wanted to help him to learn to read and to become independent.

It was to be many years later that Ricky and his mother shared with me that he not only caught up to his peers but also far exceeded them and myself in his education and college career. It was obvious that I had been part of the miracle of healing. Was I responsible? No, *God* had his hand on Ricky all along. In His plan, Ricky had to be far behind in his academics for God to work. If he had only been a year or two behind, people would not have recognized the miracle that God performed. In John 9:1–3, Jesus' disciples saw a man who had been blind from birth and asked Jesus who sinned that he had been born blind. Jesus answered that this happened so that the work of God might be displayed in his life. That is exactly what God did in Ricky's life. God is being glorified through this, not only in healing Ricky, but also by using him to teach and help others.

I am privileged to have taught Ricky and to have known the loving spirit of Jesus manifested in Ricky. But most of all, I glorify and praise Jesus for His mighty work. Our class Bible verse was Philippians 4:13, "I can do all things through Christ which strengtheneth me." Ricky proved that to be true! Praise the Lord!

MEMORIES OF A NEIGHBOR
BY VIRGINIA HARRELL

I was a neighbor of Elias, Dot and Ricky Roberts. Ricky was born with severe learning disabilities. Ricky's private school kindergarten principal had recommended that he repeat kindergarten, but he went on to first grade, which he had to repeat. I had given Ricky's mother some word and math tutoring cards, but they did not seem to help very much.

In 1970 I was a substitute teacher in a public school third grade classroom in which Ricky was a student. When I asked the class to please stand and repeat the pledge of allegiance to our flag, everyone in the class stood except Ricky. I had to say, "Ricky, you have to stand and say the pledge of allegiance." Finally, he stood up and went through the motions of the pledge of allegiance with the class. Evidently, his teachers had not pushed him to take part in class exercises, math or reading. Shortly afterward, I told his mother that she really should send him to the University Christian School's special education class.

Years later when Ricky was sixteen, he came to my house to read for me out of a sixth grade reading book. I did not think he would be able to read very much of the page, but I was amazed to hear him read the words and to attack the really difficult words in the proper manner. This was truly a miracle. I remember this vividly because I did not think he would ever be able to accomplish even this small feat.

MEMORIES OF MRS. BRUCE DUGGER

I taught a multiage special education class at University Christian School in the school year of 1977–1978. One of my students, Ricky Roberts, was a sixteen-year-old boy reading on a third grade level at that time. Most of the students had been in this class together for several years. They were like a family to one another in the midst of a world that was unkind to them. Ricky was very happy to spend a good part of his days helping the younger children learn.

I felt a heavy responsibility to teach and push Ricky to climb to higher levels. I began trying to push his reading, math and language forward. Before Christmas, I agreed with others to have him professionally tested to see what potential he could actually achieve.

His mom, Ricky and I visited Dr. Smith after the results were gathered to make an academic plan. Dr. Smith encouraged the school to let me put Ricky into some sophomore classes to see how he could cope. He was placed in world history and other subjects along with his special education class. I continued working with him on his reading, language and math skills.

Ricky did very well, and the following year he was promoted out of special education and placed in sophomore classes for credit. A lot of hard work and great perseverance found Ricky graduating with honors a few years later.

Yet I must admit, it was not Ricky alone that accomplished all of this. Ricky, as he was, could not have been able to achieve any or all of this. I beheld the visible and inner workings of God first hand! I never will forget it as long as I live.

MEMORIES OF A PRINCIPAL
BY MARGARET J. GLIDDEN

Ricky Roberts (of Jacksonville, Florida) graduated from University Christian School after attending for eight years. This young man came to the school as a nonreader with learning disabilities of a severe nature. Because he scored several grades below the classmates of his age, he was placed in a special education class when he entered the school. Although he was twelve years old and in the sixth grade, he was reading below kindergarten level. Ricky continued to work in a small, ungraded class under the direction of a special education teacher for about five years. Things appeared hopeless for Ricky, but his trust in God grew. He could not visualize graduation ahead for him and the thought of having a diploma was remote. He had resigned himself to moving along without the success that others always appeared to get. He said, "I cried to God to learn, and He taught me!"

In the winter of 1977, something out of the ordinary happened to Ricky. In December, God (at church) moved upon Ricky by His supernatural power through a preacher's laying hands upon him. He was completely and immediately healed of all his learning disabilities. Instantaneously, God filled in seven years of school (from the third grade to the tenth grade). The improvement was not due to anything that man did, but God, improving Ricky's mental capacities. At the age of sixteen, God could completely and utterly finish what He had started. If God had filled all the levels at one time, Ricky's brain would not have been able to sustain it.

MEMORIES OF ROBIN SCHOTTLEUTNER

In 1974 my husband and I took our first teaching jobs at University Christian School. I was to fill the vacancy left by the previous special education teacher, Sally Young. She had developed the program from its beginning, and since I was inexperienced, I simply tried to pick up and continue where she left off.

When I think back on that classroom of children, ages ranging from six years to sixteen years of age, I remember Ricky as a big boy sitting at his desk doing seat work with all the concentration and effort that he could muster. Though our classroom was air conditioned, he would perspire as if the calculations of his math problems were a mile run. Scholastically, he was behind his age. The reading and math problems took him long periods of time to complete. At various times, there were students Ricky's age that showed anger or embarrassment at being in the special education class.

As he progressed in school, I'm sure many noticed the growing confidence he possessed. One of the last phone conversations I had with him before we moved away showed me of his widening interests and his ability to give advice. He asked me if I had a garden, and I told him I was enjoying growing flowers. "Well," he said, "you ought to have a vegetable garden because you can eat the vegetables, but you can't eat your flowers." Though I continue to spend my time with flowers in the yard, Ricky's words still ring true.

There have been many occasions when my husband and I have spoken of Ricky's desire and determination to succeed in school. It brought us great joy to hear of his uncommon achievements

and to know he has given the glory to God. Mrs.
Roberts once asked me if I believed God could
still heal. As I look back on her question, I realize
she knew the answer to Ricky's needs rested in
God's power and ability, not in the efforts of a
teacher or in her son's desire to learn.

Notes

Introduction

1. *Tertullian Against Marcion*, 5:15.

2. John Wesley, *The Works of John Wesley*, 10:23.

3. Jonathan Edwards, *The Works of Jonathan Edwards*, 1:375.

4. Ibid, 2:261.

5. Thomas Kyd, *The Spanish Tragedy* (London: Nick Hern Books, 1997).

6. Marie Shropshire, *God Cares About Your Tears* (Eugene, OR: Harvest House Publishers, 1997), 147.

7. A. W. Tozer, *God Tells the Man Who Cares* (Camp Hill, PA: Christian Publications, 1992).

8. Marie Shropshire, *God Cares About Your Tears*, 10–11.

Chapter One
Beginnings of a Miracle

1. *Cordelle Dispatch*, May 2, 1918.

Special Education—1973–1974

Special Education—1975

Mrs. Robin Schottleutner

Ricky
Roberts

Special Education—1976

Mrs. Robin Schottleutner

Ricky
Roberts

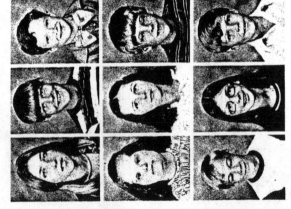

Ricky
Roberts

SOPHOMORES

Ricky
Roberts

March 27, 2000

To whom It may concern,

I knew Dr Ricky Roberts as a retarded teenage, was present the night God healed him and saw personally the after effects of such a healing.

Sincerely, *Maggie Sue Carver*
and daughter
Ruth D. Quimby

Reading level

1st 9 wks. – Pre primer level Book 2

From the back of the first report card in Special Education: This indicates that Ricky Roberts was reading below kindergarten level, although being 12 years old.

True Light Ministries Inc.

For I shall bring forth
truth out of darkness
for the sake of my people.

For more information concerning Dr. Roberts, his mother, their schedule of events, their ministry and donations to that ministry, please contact:

True Light Ministries
P.O. Box 28538
Jacksonville, FL 32218
A Non-Profit and Tax-Exempt Organization
Cell: 904-472-7786
Fax: 904-751-0304
truelightministries.org